TATTING
SECOND EDITION
DESIGNS FROM VICTORIAN LACE CRAFT

EDITED BY JULES & KAETHE KLIOT

LACIS
PUBLICATIONS
3163 Adeline Street
Berkeley, CA 94703

ISBN 0-916896-59-5

[Cover: *Tatted Bertha, late 19th C. Author's Collection*]

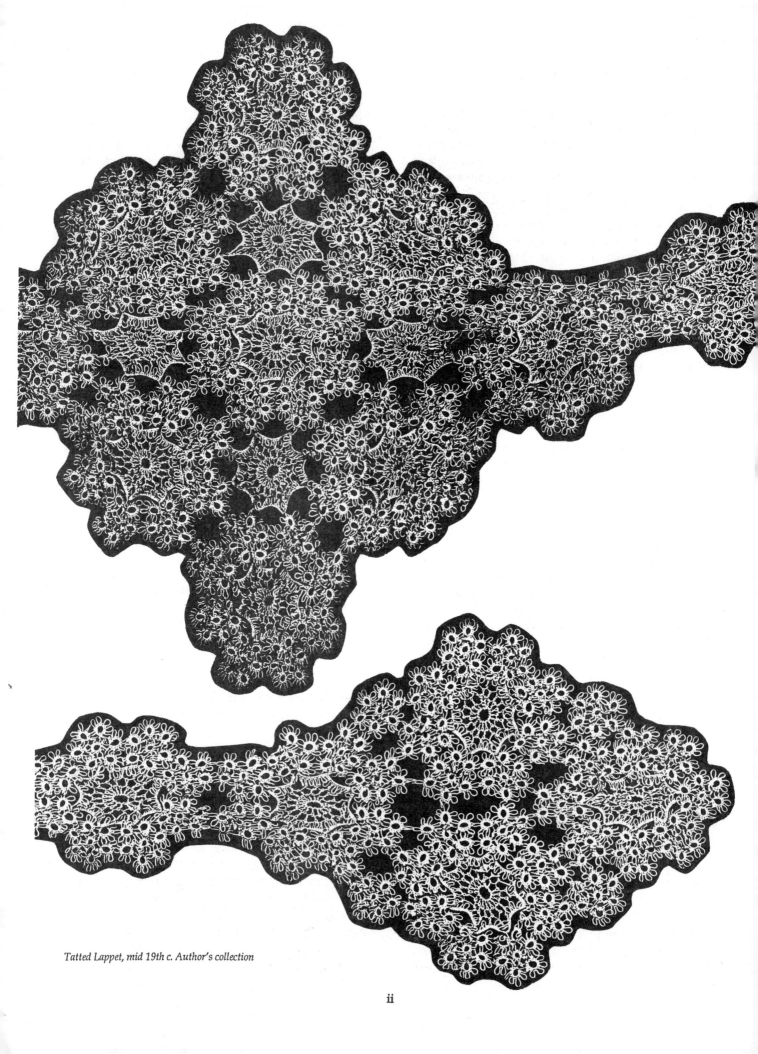

Tatted Lappet, mid 19th c. Author's collection

INTRODUCTION

Tatting is a knotted lace technique generally categorized along with other knotted techniques such as filet, macrame and Armenian lace. Essentially a half-hitch process, tatting utilizes a single strand of thread and a shuttle.

While some evidence of the technique dates back to the late 17th century in Italy where the emphasis was on knotting, its height of popularity dates to the Victorian era when it was common for both men and women to tat. Many 19th century paintings illustrate ladies of the court tatting or knotting, this being a common pastime in court and church. The tatting shuttle soon became a work of art in itself, varying in size from 1" to 8", richly ornamented and made of materials ranging from wood, ivory, bone, silver, gold and mother-of-pearl. With the compactness of the tools and ease of portability, the technique lends itself well to travel and long journeys, a probable reason for its popularity in the United States from 1850 to 1930.

In 1853, first mention is made of the picot, the simple technique that permitted in-process joining, enabling tatting to be done in one continuous process. Prior to this time, all tatted rings were sewn together after they were completed. The picot was soon explored as a decorative stitch and tatting of this period can often be identified by great delicacy, the result of numerous and long decorative picots.

Tatting is today enjoying one of its greatest revivals as evidenced by the many books recently published and reprinted exploring method and technique and the revival of *Needle Tatting* which has not only simplified the technique but allows the use of virtually any thread or yarn. The availability of virtually unlimited materials in terms of both color and weight has given rise to much exploration and artistic expression utilizing this medium, many innovations based on the most formal of the traditional designs. Many of the complex patterns found in this book can be dissected, small sections being used for new designs.

Tatting patterns are simple to follow. There are only four elements to consider when working or designing; *RINGS, CHAINS, PICOTS* and *JOININGS*. With a single shuttle, you can only make rings joined with a free thread. Most patterns will require a shuttle and ball or two shuttles. This permits the working of both rings and chains (or bars), the two major design elements. The "picot" or loop between two stitches is the other popular design element and the means by which elements are joined. The fourth element is the joining, the means by which each new ring or chain is joined to previously made sections.

Prior to working any tatting pattern, it is suggested that the design be drawn on a piece of paper, where all rings, chains and picots are shown. A number representing the number of stitches (knots) between each picot or joining should be written on this pattern. Letter each element ("A", "B", "C", etc.) to indicate the sequence in which it is worked. It will soon be obvious that a logical order is necessary if you are not to work yourself into a corner. With practice, the written instructions can be completely ignored and the patterns worked directly from the illustration. The book "THE COMPLETE BOOK OF TATTING" by Jones is an excellent reference for this graphic pattern technique, as well as for alternate working techniques including needle tatting.

NEEDLE TATTING

Although initially developed in the 1850s, this innovative technique for tatting has become the most popular tatting technique today. It not only permits the use of virtually any thread, yarn or cord but its simplicity of technique permits learning in a matter of minutes. As in crocheting and knitting, the working material is outside the work. There are no shuttles to wind and the entire working thread does not have to be carried through each stitch. Needle tatting is comparable to two shuttle tatting, where every ring and bar is knotted. Any pattern in this book which consists of knotted rings and bars can be worked with needle tatting.

This "Lacis" edition of TATTING, DESIGNS FROM VICTORIAN LACE CRAFT is an unabridged republication of five complete works printed in the early 20th century; a period when tatting was considered a fine lace art, reaching new heights of popularity and complexity. The original titles of these publications are:

THE PRISCILLA TATTING BOOK NO. 1, edited by Jessie M. DeWitt, published by the Priscilla Publishing Company, 1909.

TATTING CRAFT, MY BOOK NO. 3, by Anna Valeire, published by E. C. Spuehler, c. 1900.

TATTING DESIGNS WITH INSTRUCTIONS, BOOK NO. 5, by Adeline Cordet, published by Valley Supply Co., 1916.

FIFTEEN TATTED YOKES AND CAMISOLES FINISHED ON SATIN, BOOK 9, by Anna Valeire, published by E. C. Spuehler, c. 1900.

BOOK ON NEW AND ORIGINAL DESIGNS IN TATTING, BOOK 5, by Marie Antoinette Hees, published be E. C. Spuehler, c. 1900.

All prices and references to threads and "cordonnet" are as originally published and are generally no longer applicable. Many suitable materials are, however, readily available and can be found wherever needlework supplies are sold. In addition to "tatting thread" (a #70 or #80 cotton available in a wide variety of solid and shaded colors), pearl cotton, knitting and crochet cotton and linen lace threads make suitable materials. In general, a smooth hard material is preferred over a soft fuzzy material. Ordinary sewing thread, available in every color and shade, makes an excellent material for finer work. For the "cordonnet" a soutache braid can be used as a substitute. In needle tatting there are virtually no thread restrictions. Yarns, metallics, ribbon and bulky threads are all suitable.

BIBLIOGRAPHY

THE COMPLETE BOOK OF TATTING, Jones. describes several tatting techniques including needle tatting. All patterns presented graphically. A "must" book for any tatting enthusiast.

NEEDLE TATTING, Barbara Foster

Other tatting books by this publisher are listed on page 92.

For a complete list of titles including reprints, write publisher.

SOURCES OF SUPPLY

LACIS, 2982 Adeline St., Berkeley, CA 94703. Send $4.00 for complete catalog of books, supplies and patterns covering every aspect of tatting, as well as other lace making techniques.

CONTENTS

Tatted Cuff & Collar, c. 1930, Author's collection

PRISCILLA
Tatting Book

№ 1

Published by
The Priscilla Publishing Co.
Boston, Mass.

PRISCILLA TATTING BOOK

GENERAL DIRECTIONS

Abbreviations used: *d s*, double stitch; *p*, picot; *, repeat from preceding *; *r*, ring; *ch*, chain; *l p*, long picot; *c l*, clover-leaf.

THE MATERIALS for making tatting are a strongly twisted thread and a shuttle.

SHUTTLES. A good shuttle, one fitted in size to the hand, is necessary for the rapidity and execution of the work. The best are of black rubber, short, with wide space for thread, and close points. The silver shuttle is a delight for small work, but must oftener be refilled, the space for thread is small. The shuttle should not be wound too full, it is clumsy for working, spreads the points, and allows the thread to become roughened.

FIRST POSITION OF THE HANDS (Fig. 1). The one difficult point in learning to do tatting, is the

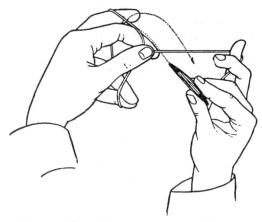

FIG. 1. FIRST POSITION OF THE HANDS

knack of the little hitch or jerk after every half stitch, which places it as a loop upon the tightened shuttle thread, on which it must slip to make a perfect stitch.

One can learn best with a firm cord or very coarse thread. (See Fig. 1 for position of the hands.) Hold the shuttle, with its sides, not edges, between the thumb and forefinger of the right hand; the thread passing under the shuttle, under three fingers, and over the little finger, then to the left hand; there with the thread-end down between the thumb and forefinger, the thread encircles all of the fingers and passes upward between the thumb and forefinger. Spread the fingers a little, to hold the thread tense, and keep the shuttle thread very tight, except at the little jerk which makes the perfect stitch.

FIRST AND SECOND POSITIONS OF THE HANDS (Figs. 1 and 2). Pass the shuttle under both threads, back over the left thread, and under the right thread. The tight upper thread on the left

hand must slip between the shuttle and forefinger going forward, and between the shuttle and thumb coming back.

After the shuttle comes back, drop the thread

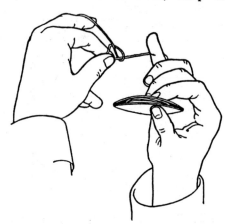

FIG. 2. SECOND POSITION OF THE HANDS

from the little finger, loosen the tight thread on the left hand by bringing the second and third fingers forward a little, and pull the shuttle thread tight with a slight jerk, then tighten the thread on the left hand with the second finger. The jerk throws a stitch on the shuttle thread, where it must slip freely, as shown in Fig. 2. Draw the shuttle thread tight, and you have the first part of the "double knot" or "double stitch," which is designated by d s, and is the common stitch in tatting.

THIRD POSITION OF THE HANDS (Fig. 3). The second part of the d s, or double stitch, made thus.

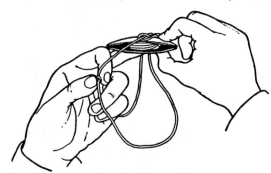

FIG. 3. THIRD POSITION OF THE HANDS

As shown in Fig. 3, pass the back end of the shuttle over and under the thread on the left hand, which slips between the shuttle and the forefinger of the right hand, in coming back. Draw the shuttle thread tight, loosen slightly the left hand, then tighten, and you have a d s, or double stitch, which should slip freely along the shuttle thread.

Do not draw the stitch too tight, but hold it

firmly. A little practise with this stitch, before going farther, will aid in acquiring the even tension which is necessary for even and accurate work.

FOURTH POSITION OF THE HANDS (Fig. 4). When the full double stitch is made, the hands return to the position of Fig. 1, ready for the next stitch.

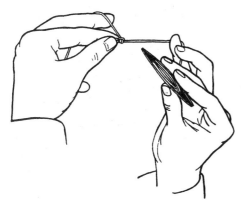

FIG. 4. FOURTH POSITION OF THE HANDS

This is shown in Fig. 4, with two finished stitches. When facility in making d s is acquired, a ring may be made of 8 or 10 d s. Pull the shuttle thread up tightly, until the first and last d s meet as closely as possible. Leave a short bit of thread between this ring and the next, and repeat the rings until they are easily made. Keeping the thread very short between the shuttle and work, adds much to the rapidity, firmness, and neatness of the work.

POSITION OF THE HANDS IN MAKING A PICOT (Fig. 5). Picots are loops around the edge of a

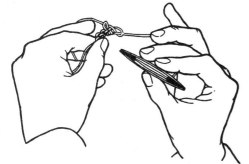

FIG. 5. POSITION OF THE HANDS IN MAKING A PICOT

ring of tatting. They add very much to the decoration and beauty of the work, make great variety possible, and are used in joining the rings and sections, thus making the work firm.

To make a picot, designated by p, merely leave a little space on the thread between two d s, finish the stitch, which holds the p in place, then pull up closely. Figure 5 shows one picot and the beginning of a second. Figure 8 shows an open picot. Figure 9 one drawn up close.

A little practise will soon give evenness in the

size of the picots. Except in a very few patterns, very long picots are not desirable, nor are many on a ring. The short ones are neater, firmer and wear better.

POSITION OF THE HANDS FOR JOINING (Fig. 6). This is done with the last picot of the ring before.

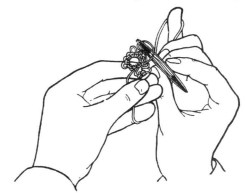

FIG. 6. POSITION OF THE HANDS FOR JOINING

Make as many d s as follow the last picot. With a pin or crochet-hook pull the thread running over the left hand, through the picot in a loop, through which pass the shuttle, and draw tight. Finish the ring, and you have two joined rings.

TATTING WITH SHUTTLE AND BALL (Fig. 7). There are very few tatting designs now which use

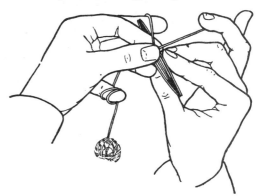

FIG. 7. TATTING WITH SHUTTLE AND BALL

but one thread. Most of them are made with the shuttle and ball, a very few with two shuttles.

It is often helpful to estimate the amount of shuttle thread required for the design in hand, and wind it upon the shuttle. This is done by allowing one yard to six ordinary rings of fourteen d s, and a little over to run through the chains. With coarse thread a little more is needed.

Do not detach the shuttle thread from the ball. Rings are made with the shuttle only, chains with shuttle and ball. To work with the shuttle and ball (see Fig. 7), make a ring with the shuttle, turn it down and hold tightly between the thumb and forefinger of the left hand. Pass the ball thread over the left fingers, and wind it several times around the lower part of the little finger. With the shuttle make d s as for a ring, drawing them up closely to the ring. Turn and make another

FIG. 8. OPEN PICOT

ring, joining it to the first. Turn and repeat the chain. Join all very closely.

FIG. 9. CLOSED PICOT

JOINING THREADS. The "weaver's knot" is often used, but a simpler one is very reliable.

Tie as for a common knot, but be careful that the second tie lies exactly across the first; one thread forming a loop under the two ends of the other, and the other looping over the two ends of the one.

FIG. 10. SINGLE OR HALF KNOT. SMALL JOSEPHINE PICOT

FIG. 11. SINGLE OR HALF KNOTS. LARGE JOSEPHINE PICOT

Pull evenly the two ends together, with each hand very tightly, and you will have a firm knot. A drop of water on the ends before tying will firmly fasten the most wiry thread.

JOSEPHINE KNOTS OF SINGLE OR HALF STITCHES (Figs. 10 and 11). The Josephine knot is a ring made with the shuttle alone, and with only the first half of the stitch, or d s. It is most frequently made of four or five, or of eight half stitches, but may be made of ten or more. It is a very pretty addition, and is often useful for joining in elaborate designs. In many German patterns these knots are used profusely with fine effect, and serve to join figures, which without them must be made separately and joined on. Clusters of very tiny knots make a pleasing variety.

SUGGESTIONS TO THE BEGINNER. Do not be discouraged by a ring which will not slip, or a false stitch. The best experts of long experience find false stitches and mistakes to rip out.

One very rapid expert keeps the pin for joining and ripping, on a tape around her neck, hanging just the right length to use quickly.

A very plain pattern, by a slight change, can be transformed into a thing of beauty, and a joy to create. Figure 13 made with No. 60 D. M. C., the thread between rings very short; every other ring on one side larger, 3 d s, 10 p's separated by 2 d s,

3 d s, is a beautiful and useful edging, which may be curved, shaped, or widened indefinitely.

Some simplest patterns made smaller and finer, are beautiful for handkerchiefs. As Fig. 14, with 2 d s instead of 3 d s, made of No. 60 or 70 mercerized thread.

Make as few joinings in the thread as possible.

Knots may sometimes be hidden under a few d s thrown over them when making a chain.

Rings are always made with one thread, chains with two. Picots are of ordinary length unless a long picot (1 p) is indicated. When the directions say "r 3 p separated by 2 d s," or ch the same it means 2 d s, p, 2 d s, p, 2 d s, p, 2 d s; that is, there must be as many d s before the first p and after the last as there are between; but if they say r, or ch, 3 d s, 3 p's separated by 2 d s, 3 d s, it means 3 d s, p, 2 d s, p, 2 d s, p, 3 d s.

A clover-leaf is a group of three rings made close together.

When a ring or other part is to be repeated three times, it means that you are to make that part three times, not counting the one already made, so that there will be four when finished.

It will be well for the beginner to practise on the simple edges and insertions which follow, before attempting the more intricate patterns.

FIGURE 12. EDGING. This is the simple edge our

FIG. 12. EDGING

grandmothers made, and it is very dainty when made with fine thread and used on the edge of footing to trim handkerchiefs, or made of coarser thread is suitable for edging ruffles for underwear and children's clothing. It may be made with any number of stitches between picots, and with two or more picots if desired. To make like illustration, r 3 p separated by 3 d s (3 d s, p, 3 d s, p, 3 d s, p, 3 d s, close), leave one-fourth inch of thread, repeat r, joining by 1st p to last p in preceding r. Repeat indefinitely.

FIGURE 13. DOUBLE ROW OF RINGS. This may be used as an edge or as an insertion with the simple

FIG. 13. DOUBLE ROW OF RINGS

4

edge. Ring 3 p separated by 3 d s, turn, leave one-fourth inch thread, repeat r, * turn, leave one-fourth inch thread, r joined by 1st p to last p of 1st r, turn, leave one-fourth inch thread, r joined by 1st p to last p of 2d r. Repeat from star indefinitely.

FIGURE 14. EDGE MADE WITH TWO THREADS. Ring 3 p separated by 3 d s. Take the spool thread

FIG. 14. EDGE MADE WITH TWO THREADS

as directed above and ch 4 d s, p, 4 d s. Drop spool thread, turn, and repeat r. joining as in simple edge.

FIGURE 15. INSERTION TO MATCH FIG. 14. Make

FIG. 15. INSERTION TO MATCH FIG. 14

an edge like the last, then a 2d row, joining each ring to a p of a r in the 1st row.

FIGURE 16. CLOVER LEAF EDGE. * Ring 3 p separated by 3 d s, close; close up r 3 d s, join to last p in 1st r, 3 d s, 3 p separated by 1 d s, 3 d s, p, 3 d s,

FIG. 16. CLOVER LEAF EDGE

close; close up, r 3 d s, join to last p in 2d r, 2 p separated by 3 d s, 3 d s, close. Chain 4 d s, 3 p separated by 2 d s, 4 d s, turn. Repeat from star.

Figs. 17, 18, 19. Waist Front and Yoke

MATERIALS.—Nos. 50 and 150 thread. Two shuttles are necessary. For convenience' sake call one shuttle A and the other B.

Join the two threads.

1st round—With shuttle A r 1 d s, 12 l p separated by 2 d s, 1 d s, close and tie the two threads together.

2d round—Put thread B round the left-hand fingers, holding it between thumb and 1st finger. With shuttle A ch 2 d s, 1 p, 1 d s, p, 1 d s, 1 p, 2 d s. Fasten to first p below. Repeat 11 times.

3d round—Pass both threads up on the under side and fasten by slipping shuttle A through loop of thread B drawn through last p of 12th scallop and also 1st p of 1st scallop of round previous. Put thread B round the fingers and with shuttle A ch 3 d s, p, 2 d s. Drop shuttle A and with shuttle B r 7 p separated by 1 d s, close. These picots should be graded in length, commencing short, increasing to 4th and decreasing again. Drop shuttle B, but keep thread B round the fingers and with shuttle A ch 2 d s, p, 3 d s. Join to 3d p of 1st scallop· and 1st p of 2d scallop of previous round. Repeat 11 times, tie threads together and trim close.

With fine needle and 150 thread work around the edge of the wheel. The stitch required is made by putting needle behind the thread into picot, then throwing the thread from the needle to the left under the needle. When the needle is drawn through the loop thus made it ties a hard knot. Commence with the 2d p of any outer r, working into each p, and leaving thread enough between the p's to make a slight outward curve. After the last p of the r, simply slip the needle through the 2 short p's below, running the needle from right to left so that the thread crosses itself, tie into 1st p of next r, back into curved thread between the last 2 p's of previous ring, and then back into 2d p of 2d r, 3d p, and so on. Continue in this

FIG. 17. WAIST FRONT. SEE FIG. 18.

5

way around the wheel, which will now lie flat and show its beauty.

Make 46 wheels.

From some dark, stiff stuff, as cambric or silk, cut a pattern, which need not be too exact, of a

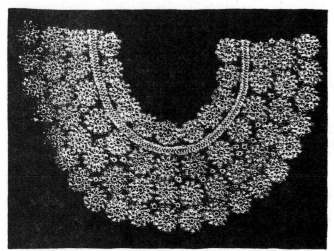

FIG. 19. DRESS YOKE. SEE FIG. 18

pointed dress front, hollowing out the neck to fit. Pin one wheel in the pointed end. Above it, not quite touching it, pin two with two outside rings adjoining each other but not quite touching. Pin three in 3d row, placing middle one in straight line above the first one in the point. Increase the number of wheels in each row by one until eight wheels stand in the row at the neck. Let each interior wheel be in a straight line with the wheel in second line below. Pin three wheels, and then two, in the two rows on each side the neck.

Make 62 simple rings of 1 d s, 12 l p separated by 2 d s, 1 d s, like the centre of the wheels, and pin a ring in the centre of the vacant space between each two wheels.

Commencing, we will suppose, with the 2d row of

FIG. 18. DETAIL OF FIGS. 17 AND 19

2 wheels, with needle and thread tie into upper edge of left-hand wheel lying nearest the right-hand wheel, cross to right-hand wheel, back to left, and thus continue as long as the wheels are near enough to allow stitches of uniform length. Then follow down the edge of either wheel until the simple ring can be reached, going on around this, fastening it to the wheel you are on, and then to the bottom wheel and around to the other wheel, then upward, and so on until you have filled the whole space between the 3 wheels with stitches of as uniform length as possible. Thus work the 46 wheels into one solid piece of "all over." The stitch needs no extra fastening, but the thread can be cut anywhere, and a new piece can be joined on in the manner described in the General Directions whenever it seems too short to be handy. Should the wheels at the neck make too irregular an edge, insert simple rings, large or small as required.

For a stock collar to go with this front, cut a pattern out of cambric to fit the neck, make 26 or 28 wheels, according to the size of the collar, with 12 or 13 rings to go between, pin them on the pattern in two rows and work all together.

The round dress yoke illustrated in Fig. 19 may be made by following the directions given for the waist front. The wheels are worked in the same way, and the collar, when finished, shows a very effective piece of tatting.

FIG. 20. DETAIL OF FIG. 21

Fig. 21. Centrepiece with Insertion

MATERIALS.—For this insertion use coarse crochet cotton.

Two threads are used. With 1 thread * 1 6 d s, p, 2 d s, 3 p separated by 1 d s, 4 d s, close; close up, r 4 d s, join to last p of 1st r, 2 d s, 5 p separated by 1 d s, 2 d s, p, 4 d s, close; close up, r 4 d s, join to last p of 2d r, 2 p separated by 1 d s, 2 d s, p, 4 d s, close. With two threads, ch 4 d s, p, 4 d s. Repeat 3 times, joining the c l's by 1st and last p's, and the ch's to the p of 1st ch. Join squares as seen in illustration, baste carefully on linen, buttonhole carefully and cut out cloth underneath.

Fig. 22. Border for Doily

MATERIALS.—No. 36 thread, 1 skein of floss, and a small piece of net.

Begin with the wheel, made thus: 12 p's, separated by 1 d s, close, tie, and cut the thread;

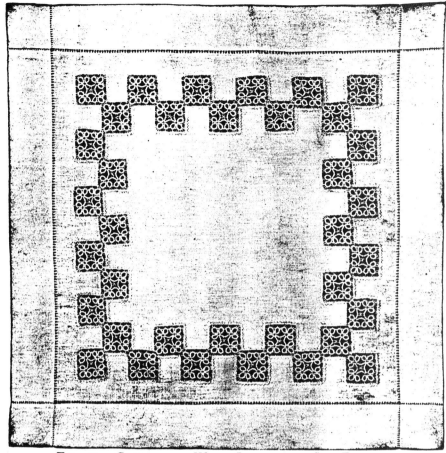

FIG. 21. CENTREPIECE WITH INSERTION. SEE FIG. 20

The wheel which forms most of the border is made thus: r 12 p separated by 2 d s, close, tie and cut the thread; r 6 d s, join to a p of the r, 6 d s, close, turn; leave about ¼ inch of thread, r 4 d s, 7 p separated by 2 d s, 4 d s, close, turn; make another small r, and continue the large and small r's alternately until you have 12 of each, joining each small one to a p of the centre, and the large ones to each other by the 1st p. Make 40 of these wheels for the border, joining them as seen in the illustration, and in the open spaces make four-leaved figures, each r of 4 d s, 5 p separated by 2 d s, 4 d s, close, and join them to the wheels by the middle p's of the r's. Along the inner edge of the border make a double row of r's, each of 7 d s, 7 p separated by 2 d s, 7 d s, close, each row of r's joined by the 1st p, and the outer row joined to the wheels and four-leaved figures. Hemstitch a small square of the linen to fit the centre, and sew the tatting on carefully with fine thread, catching each p on the edge. Press the work with a damp cloth over it.

r 2 d s, p, 2 d s, join to p of r, 2 d s, p, 2 d s, close, turn, leave one-fourth inch of thread, r 4 d s, 5 p separated by 3 d s, 4 d s, close, turn, make another small r. Alternate the large and small r's until 12 of each are made, joining large ones to each other by the 1st p.

Make 8 of the wheels, then put them together, by the rows of r's and ch's, thus; the r is same as large one in wheel, beginning with 7 d s instead of 4; and ch is of 4 d s, 5 p separated by 2 d s, 4 d s. The ch at the turn has 11 p. Alternate the r's and ch's, joining 10 of the ch's to each wheel, and 4 r's to 4 on opposite side. as seen in illustration. Place the square of net over one of thin lawn, then baste the tatting on. Buttonhole the inner edge with the silk, then cut out.

Fig. 23. Border for Handkerchief

MATERIALS.—One-fourth yard of fine linen, and No. 80 lace thread with No. 100 thread for the hemstitching.

This handkerchief design may be adapted for other articles. A centrepiece may be made by using coarse thread for the lace and heavy linen for the centre. Two of the corners would make handsome tie ends; the tie could be made of fine net or mull.

FIG. 22. BORDER FOR DOILY

FIG. 23. BORDER FOR HANDKERCHIEF

* r 6 d s, join to middle p of 1st ch on upper part, 6 d s, close, ch 6 d s, join to a p of one of the centre r's, ch 1 d s, 9 p separated by 2 d s, 1 d s, join to p at opposite side of centre r; turn, ch 5 d s, p, 5 d s, turn, r 6 d s, join to 2d p of ch, 6 d s, close, ch 3 p separated by 2 d s, r joined to 4th p, ch 5 p separated by 2 d s, r joined to 6th p; repeat the 2d ch, r joined to 8th p, repeat the 1st ch, join to p of centre r. Repeat the ch of 9 p, joining by middle p to middle p of 3d ch on upper part, and at end to p of centre r, ch 6 d s. Repeat from * joining the scallops by p of 1st and last ch's.

Fig. 25. Tie End

MATERIALS.—No. 40 thread, 1 skein of silk, and ¼ yard of net.

The wheel which forms the end is made thus: 12 p separated by 1 d s, tie and cut threads; then r 3 p separated by 3 d s, joining to centre by

Fig. 24. Trimming

Make a double row of r's, each of 3 p separated by 3 d s, with three-eighths inch of thread between and joined by 1st and last p's, as long as you desire the trimming to be. Join shuttle thread to p of 1st r and ch 1 d s, 3 p separated by 2 d s, 1 d s, join to next r: repeat to end and also on other side of double row of r's. For the lower part make the r's for the centres of the scallops 1st, each of 11 d s, p, 12 d s, p, 1 d s, close, tie and cut. With single thread

FIG. 24. TRIMMING

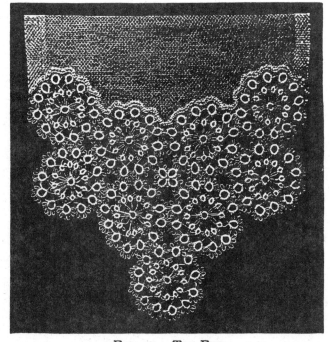

FIG. 25. TIE END

8

middle p. Leave one-fourth inch of thread, r 7 d s, 7 p separated by 2 d s, 7 d s, close. Alternate the large and small r's until 12 of each are made, joining the large ones to each other by the 1st p, and small ones to the centre. Make 9 wheels for each end, joining them by large r's, as seen in the illustration. In the centre is a four-leaved figure,

Fig. 26. Centrepiece

MATERIAL.—No. 40 thread.

This piece will be most easily understood by studying its different parts in detail; these may be termed rosettes, clover leaves, ring (midway between centre and border), insertion (between the

FIG. 26. CENTREPIECE

each r of 7 d s, 5 p separated by 3 d s, 7 d s, close.

Make the tie the required length (the model is one and three-fourths yards long) and hem the edges. Place a small piece of lawn under the net at each end. Baste the tatting on the net, and buttonhole the edge with silk. Cut the lawn and net from the edge.

Tatting, No. 1

rosettes in corners of border), medallions, and edge.

ROSETTES. 1. * Ring 5 d s, p, 5 d s, close. Repeat from * 4 times close together, tie and cut. *2d round*—* Ring 5 p separated by 2 d s, close. Repeat r, joining to 1st r by 1st p, and to p of one of the central r's. Repeat from * around wheel. *3d round*—Without cutting thread join in p between 2 r's, ch 2 d s, 7 p separated by 1 d s, 2 d s, join between next 2 r's. Repeat around rosette. Make 9 of these rosettes. For rosette in centre, let r's and scallops be 9 instead of 10, and middle p of each scallop be quite long.

2. In circle and edge, r 7 p separated by 2 d s, close; tie threads together so as to form 8th p, and work 2d and 3d rows as before, with only 8 r's and scallops, however. Make 18 of these.

CLOVER LEAVES. These are of 3 lobes made alike; r 5 d s, 5 p separated by 2 d s, 5 d s, close, tie and cut. The joinings are somewhat intricate, and require careful attention. The first whorl of leaves simply joins middle p of 1st lobe to middle p of each scallop of central rosette, but the other joinings generally follow these principles. (a) Whenever a single lobe is to be joined to a single lobe or scallop directly opposite, its middle p and next p on left or right, according as loop to be joined is on left or right, is joined to middle p and p to left or right of the other. (b) Whenever a single lobe is to be joined to 2 lobes, the 1st two outside p's of the single lobe are joined to 3d and 2d p of one of the 2 lobes, and the last two outside p's of the single lobe to the 4th and 3d p of the other. Thus, the 1st lobe of 2d whorl of leaves joins its 1st and 2d p to 3d and 2d p of 2d lobe of 1st whorl of leaves, and its 4th and 5th p to 4th and 3d p of 2d lobe of next leaf; but the 2d lobe as an exception joins 3d and 4th p to 5th and 4th p of a scallop of one of 9 central rosettes. The 3d lobe also joins 2d and 3d p to 2d and 1st p of a scallop of another rosette. If a rosette has been already joined, skip one scallop.

The 3 leaves between rosettes and r follow rule (a); for that between the single lobe and two lobes, rule (b). Join 2d and 3d leaves to adjacent scallops of rosette. The joinings to the rosettes in r are to the same scallops from which straight lines of tatting start.

Of the leaves between medallions and insertion, the lobes in the corners are joined to the same scallops of rosettes from which straight lines of tatting start. These leaves follow rule (a) except that the single leaves inside join only middle p to middle p of 4th r of insertion from either corner, and to 4th p or 2d p of lobe above or below, the joinings to medallion are regular, using alternate scallops, except that lowest leaf joins to scallop next to the one above; the 3d lobe of last leaf is free.

Of the 5 leaves between medallion and edge, the 2 single ones on left and right join middle p to 4th or 2d p of 2d scallop from those joined to leaves last mentioned (those between medallion and insertion), and next p to left or right to 2d or 4th of next scallop. The 2d and 3d lobes join

each two adjacent p's to the 4 p's of 5th, 6th, 7th loops from corners. Of the 3 inner leaves, the upper lobes are joined regularly to the scallops of medallion next to those to which the outside are joined, leaving 2 scallops free, while the lower lobes are joined to 4 r's of straight line of tatting on each side of the one in the point, which also is free.

RING. Ring 5 d s, p, 5 d s, close. Make 4 of these r's close together. Tie thread ends together and twist so that the 4 make an X, and cut; make 36 of these (4 between the rosettes). Tie thread to last p of a rosette scallop, * r 2 d s, join to next p of same scallop, 3 p separated by 2 d s, 2 d s, close, join to p of X. Repeat r, joining to 1st, join to next p of X. Repeat from * 3 times. Make another r, joining by last p to 4th p of scallop of another rosette. Fasten thread to last p of rosette and cut. Turn work around and make outer straight line in same way, except that the r has 5 p instead of 4. Make 9 sections.

INSERTION. Make 27 X's in same way; r 2 d s, p, 2 d s, join to 2d p of scallop left free between previous joinings of rosette, 3 p separated by 2 d s, 2 d s, close. Repeat r, joining to 1st, join to p of an X. Continue using 3 X's and joining the 9th r by the last p to 2d p of a scallop of one of the border rosettes. Turn work, and make other side in same way.

MEDALLIONS. Ring 5 d s, 5 p separated by 2 d s, 5 d s, close. Make 4 close together, tie and cut; 3 p separated by 2 d s, close, turn, r 3 d s, 4 p separated by 2 d s, 3 d s, close. All these r's should be joined to preceding ones by 1st p. Make 22 in each row, joining 1st, 2d, 3d, and 12th, 13th, 14th of inner row, to 2d, 3d, and 4th p of opposite central r's. Tie on thread of spool to 1st p of 1st r of outer row. Make a chain of 7 p separated by 1 d s. Join to last p of same r, and then into 1st of 2d. Continue around the medallion.

EDGE. Twelve X's are needed between each 2 rosettes, 108 in all. Tie into 1st p of 2d scallop to right of one joined to insertion; r 2 d s, join to last p of scallop between, 3 p separated by 2 d s, close; join to p of X. Make 27 r's, each joined to preceding one by 1st p, leaving 2 between 1st two and last two X's. The outer row contains 24 r's each of 3 d s, 5 p separated by 2 d s, 3 d s, close. After 5th r join to 2 p's in succession of an X; after 12th omit joining, after 19th join to both r's of X. Finish as usual in 2d scallop from beginning. Tie thread of spool to 1st p of last line. Make chain of 5 p separated by 2 d s; tie to last p of r below, and then into 1st p of next r; join these scallops to each other by 1st p, repeat for each r below.

10

Fig. 27. Collar

MATERIAL.—No. 70 thread.

All rings consist of 6 d s, p, 6 d s, close; all chains of 6 d s, p, 6 d s. The outside row is made first. *1st row*—Ring, ch, * r, joined to 1st r, then another r as close to the last as possible. Now pass the spool thread up between the two r's and the shuttle under it towards you and make a ch. Repeat from * till you have 4 ch's; r joined to last r, ch, r joined into same p as the last one, making a group of 3 r's, which forms the corner; another r close up, then a ch, and repeat until long enough for the collar, forming the second corner like the first. When you have completed 4 groups of r's at the end make a ch and continue with *2d row*—Ring, joined to same p as last r, ch, r, join to same p, making a group of 4 r's. Pass the shuttle thread under the spool thread

FIG. 27. COLLAR

FIG. 28. STOCK COLLAR. SEE FIG. 29

towards you and make another r close up, joining it to the next group. So continue till you have completed 3 groups, then, without passing the shuttle under, make a r close up, joined to corner group of 3, then another r close up, joined to next group, ch joined to last ch. Repeat to end of row where the last ch is tied at point of beginning. *3d row*—Ring, ch joined to 1st inside ch, r joined to last r, pass thread up as in 1st row. Complete two groups, then make another r close up, joined to the p which joins the corner ch's in 2d row, ch, r joined to last group, forming a group of 3, and repeat to end. *4th row*—Like 2d row. *5th row*—Tie thread into p which joins corner ch's, ch, r, joined to next ch in 4th row. Repeat to end.

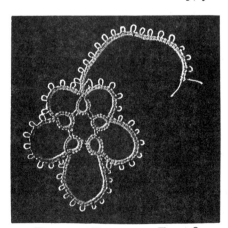

FIG. 29. DETAIL OF FIG. 28

Fig. 28. Stock Collar

MATERIAL.—No. 100 thread.

This collar is composed of 23 flower-like figures. A r consists of 6 d s, 1 p, 4 d s, 1 p, 6 d s, close.

A figure is made thus: r, ch 5 p separated by 3 d s, r, joining by 1st p to last p of preceding r, ch 8 p, r, ch 12 p, r, ch 8 p, r, joining to 4th and 1st r's and thus forming a circle; ch 5 p, join to top of 1st r. Chain 16 p and make another figure, joining 3d p of 1st ch to 4th p of 4th ch in 1st figure, and 3d p of 2d ch to 4th p of 3d ch in 1st figure. Join the 3d figure to the 3d p of 4th ch in 2d figure by the 4th p of 2d ch, and to the 2d p of 5th ch in 2d figure by the 4th p of 3d ch.

Repeat the 3d figure 3 times, then reverse by joining the 4th p of 1st ch to 4th p of 5th ch and the 3d p of 2d ch to 3d p of 4th ch. Make 4 more figures, joining like the 2d to the 1st, when you will have 11 figures. Join the 12th like the 3d to the 2d and finish, merely reversing the order. Then fill in the point, using two figures, ch's and cl's arranged as in the illustration. One advantage of this design is that it is worked continuously without breaking the thread except for filling in the point.

Fig. 30. Border for Handkerchief

MATERIAL.—No. 100 thread.

1st row—Ring 12 p separated by 2 d s, close, and then make (a little distance from this r), * 6 d s, join in a p of last r, 6 d s, close; a little distance from this r, 4 d s, 6 p separated by 2 d s, 4 d s, close. Repeat from * 11 times, joining the 12th and 1st r's in each row, tie and cut. Make enough of these wheels to go around the handkerchief, joining and turning the corner as shown in the illustration. Eight wheels on a side makes a very good-sized handkerchief.

2d row—Ring 4 d s, 7 p separated by 2 d s, 5 d s, close. Make a double row of these r's to form an insertion along the inner side of the wheels. Fasten them to the wheels, as shown in the illustration, by joining the two middle p's of a wheel to two r's of the insertion, then leaving 3 r's on the same edge of the insertion that are

11

not joined to the wheels, and joining the next 2 until the corner is reached. Fasten a wheel in the corner, made as follows: r 6 d s, 8 p separated by 2 d s, 6 d s, close, r 6 d s, fasten to the last p of the other r, 2 d s, 7 p separated by 2 d s, 6 d s, close. Make 2 more of these r's, joining the last to the 1st in the form of a wheel. Then make a row of insertion the rest of the way around, putting the small wheels in the corners.

3d row—Like 2d row, except that the insertion is put on the outside row of wheels.

4th row—Make a row of half wheels for the outer edge as follows: 1 d s, 7 p separated by 2 d s, 3 d s, fasten to the middle p of the r directly opposite the middle of a wheel, 2 d s, close; make (a little distance from this r) 6 d s, fasten in first p of r, 3 d s, join to middle p of next r of insertion, 3 d s, close, make (a little distance from this r) 4 d s, fasten to middle p of next r of insertion, 6 p separated by 2 d s, 4 d s, close. Continue until you have 7 large and 7 small r's, fastening the last to the insertion, then break off thread. Make one of these half wheels opposite each whole wheel, only at the corners they should contain 9 r's instead of 7.

FIG. 30. BORDER FOR HANDKERCHIEF

Fig. 31. Doily

1st row—* Ring 5 p separated by 2½ d s, close, ch 5 p separated by 2½ d s. Repeat from * 7 times, joining the r's by 2d and 4th p's, tie and cut.

The r's in 2d row around wheel are made like those in the wheel; the ch's have 3 p separated by 3 d s, and are joined by their middle p to the preceding row.

FIG. 31. DOILY

3d row—Ring like others, ch 3 p separated by 5 d s, joining by middle p to preceding row but leaving the r's free.

4th row—Make 8 wheels like centre one, but with 9 r's and ch's instead of 8 and joining them as seen in the illustration.

The *5th row* is made like 1st, and joined as seen in illustration. Make 6th row same as last.

7th row—Ring 5 p separated by 2½ d s, ch 5 p separated by 3 d s. Join the r's to those of the 6th row by the 2d and 4th p of each. *Last row*—Ring 7 p separated by 2 d s, close, and leave about ⅛ of an inch of thread, r 3 p separated by 2 d s, attaching middle p to 2d on ch of wheel; again leave ⅛ inch of thread, repeat small r, attaching 1st p to 1st on large r. Make another small r and attach to 4th p of ch on wheel, making three small r's between large ones, and so continue around the wheel.

A pretty doily may be made by substituting fine linen or lawn for the tatted centre illustrated.

Fig. 32. Chemise Yoke

MATERIAL.—No. 100 thread.

Begin and end each r and ch with 2 d s, unless otherwise directed. Make the band in four strips. Commence with a ch of 20 d s, turn, r 7 p separated by 2 d s. Repeat ch's and r's till you have 18 r's for the 2 front pieces and 15 r's for the back pieces. Tie the 2 threads together at the end, then turn, leave p at end, and over each ch make another ch of 11 p separated by 2 d s, joining in top of r between scallops of 1st row. Tie threads together at the end and leave enough thread to fasten to the other figure when ready. Make another row of the edging and connect with the 1st row with ch's of 10 d s each, fastening to each r alternating between the 2 edges. Leave a p or threads long enough to tie to other figures when ready.

To Make the Wheels.—Make centre r of 10 1 p separated by 3 d s, close and tie. * Ring 7 p separated by 2 d s, fastening centre p to a p of centre r, ch 20 d s. Repeat from * 9 times. Without cutting thread ch 4 d s, 11 p separated by 2 d s, 4 d s, join in the top of next r and repeat around wheel. Join the wheels in groups of 3, making 4 groups.

Tie spool and shuttle-thread into the centre r at side of one of the 2 wheels, between 2 of the

of edging has 20 r s. Two ch's of 10 d s, joining the edging should be joined to each of the 5 r's at the end of the V, and at the centre fasten 3 r's of the outer edge together. To this fasten the figure at the end of V, which is a wheel with chain figures on 3 sides. Trim the armholes with one row of the edging, and the zigzag ch's, leaving a p on the points to sew on by. Do not draw the shuttle-thread as tight as for scallops.

Finish the top of chemise as in Battenberg work, sew on the tatting by two or three picots on a scallop, run the needle under the braid to the next scallop. Do not sew very firmly, as the tatted yoke

FIG. 32. CHEMISE YOKE
SEE FIG. 33

scallops. Chain 6 d s, 51 p separated by 2 d s, 6 d s, fasten at same place. Chain 6 d s, 29 p separated by 2 d s, 6 d s, fasten to side of long ch at the 15th p, tie and cut threads. Tie threads into same place as before. Chain 6 d s, 29 p separated by 2 d s, fasten to 15th p on the other side of the long ch, tie and cut threads.

Fasten shuttle thread into 3d p of one of the side ch's, r 7 p separated by 2 d s, close. Make 8 of these r's, fastening by the shuttle-thread to the p's of the side ch, skipping 2 or more as necessary. Make 6 r's across the top of the long ch and 8 on the other side ch. Repeat this figure at the side of opposite wheel. Then tie one end of one of the 2 pieces of insertion made for the back of the yoke to each end of the figure where the side bars are fastened to the long one.

Make the shoulder pieces the same with a bar-figure added to the lower side of the 3d wheel, and fasten on the other end of the insertion for back. Make front of yoke same as back, and make insertion like the band to form the V. Make inside edge with 13 r's, fastening 3d and 4th scallop at each side of 3d wheel. The outer row

can be worn longer than the garment without laundering, and should be removed from garment when washed, and when necessary to launder the yoke should be done separately, wrapping over a bottle and cheese-cloth basted over it. Put in cold suds, boil twenty minutes, suds, rinse, and dry on the bottle or fruit-jar, then remove and press under a damp cloth, and the work is preserved, otherwise it will be ruined.

Fig. 34. Collar

MATERIALS.—Two spools of thread No. 40, half a yard of fishnet, and two skeins of Caspian floss, and half a yard of thin India linen.

The border is formed of oval-shaped sections and wheels. For the oval, begin with a r of 8 p separated by 2 d s. Then 3 d s, p, 3 d s, join to a p of the r, 3 d s, p, 3 d s, close, join on the 2d thread and ch 4 d s, 5 p separated by 2 d s, 4 d s. Repeat 7 times, joining each r to a p of the centre. Make a c l, each r of 7 d s, 5 p separated by 2 d s, 7 d s, close, joining 2 of the r's to 2 ch's of the wheel. Around the wheel and c l make a row of r's and ch's, each r of 4 d s, p, 4 d s, join to p of wheel, 4 d s, p, 4 d s, close; ch the same as in the wheel. Make 17 of the ovals, joining to each other by middle p's of 2 ch's as seen in the illustration. Make 15 wheels for the inner edge of the collar, joining them to each other by 2 ch's, and at the ends to the ovals with c l's between.

Baste the net over the India linen, and on it mark the shape of the collar, taking the pattern from a lace design, or by cutting a paper pattern the desired shape.

Baste the tatting carefully in place, and with the floss buttonhole-stitch to the net and linen, using the long-and-short stitch.

Doily
NOT ILLUSTRATED.

MATERIAL.—Crochet cotton, No. 50.

This is a round doily about 12 inches in diameter. It has a 6½-in. centre with a border composed of 11 2½-in. wheels. Commence with a wheel for the centre and make a four-ringed figure thus: r d s, 5 p separated by 2 d s, 6 d s, close. Repeat three times, tie, and cut thread. Now make a c l thus: * r 4 p separated by 3 d s, close, r 4 p separated by 4 d s, joining by 1st p to last p in 1st r, close, r like the 1st, joined by 1st p to 2d r. Chain 4 d s, 3 p separated by 3 d s, 4 d s. Repeat from * 7 times, joining each alternate ch by middle p to middle p of a r in the central figure, and joining the c l's together by the middle p's in the side r's. Tie the threads to the loose ends at the beginning of row and cut. Now tie the shuttle thread into a right-hand p of a middle r in a c l and * ch 2 d s, 5 p separated by 4 d s, 2 d s, join to 1st p in middle r of next c l, 2 d s, p, 2 d s, join to next p. Repeat from * 7 times, draw both threads through 1st p in last row and * ch 2 d s, p, 2 d s, join to next p. Repeat from * around wheel, tie and cut.

1st row around wheel—Make a c l, ch 4 d s, join to a p in edge of wheel, ch 4 d s, join to next p, ch 4 d s, join to next p, ch 4 d s, c l joining to last as in the wheel. Repeat around the wheel, tie and cut.

2d row—Make like next to last row in the wheel except that there are only 4 p's between the c l's.

3d and 4th rows—Like last row in wheel.

5th row—Like 1st except that the p's in ch's are separated by 5 d s and the ch's are joined by middle p's only, skipping first 1 p and then 2, in 4th row.

6th row—Like 2d except that there are but 3 p's between c l's.

7th row—Like 3d.

For the border make 11 wheels like the one in the centre, joining them to each other by the 2 middle p's in the 1st and 6th scallops, and to the doily by the 6 p's which are midway between those which join the wheels together, skipping 6 p's in the edge of doily between the 1st and 2d, 2d and 3d, 4th and 5th, 5th and 6th, 7th and 8th, 8th and 9th, 10th and 11th wheels, and 5 p's between the 3d and 4th, 6th and 7th, 9th and 10th, 11th and 1st wheels.

Edging
NOT ILLUSTRATED.

Two shuttles are used in making this edge. The 2d shuttle is used the same as a spool in making ch's.

Chain 7 p separated by 3 d s, with 2d shuttle r 3 d s, 7 p separated by 2 d s, 3 d s, close, ch 5

FIG. 33. DETAIL OF FIG. 32. FULL SIZE

d s, with 1st shuttle r like last, ch 6 d s, r 3 d s, 6 p separated by 2 d s, 3 d s, close, ch 8 d s, r 3 d s, 6 p separated by 2 d s, 3 d s, close, ch 6 d s, r 3 d s, 7 p separated by 2 d s, 3 d s, close, ch 5 d s, with 2d shuttle r 3 d s, 3 p separated by 2 d s, join to 1st r made, 3 p separated by 2 d s, 3 d s, close. Repeat as many times as desired. A crocheted heading may be added if desired.

FIG. 34. COLLAR. SEE FIG. 35.

Fig. 36. Yoke

MATERIAL.—No. 36 thread.

Begin with a square of 4 c l's made thus: r 7 d s, 5 p separated by 3 d s, 7 d s, close and make two more r's joining them by the 1st p. Join the 2d thread and ch 15 d s, p, 15 d s. Turn and make another c l like the 1st, turn, ch 15 d s, fasten to p of the 1st ch, ch 15 d s, turn, make another c l, then another ch joined to the centre p, then the 4th c l and another ch. Join the c l's to each other by the 2d p of the 1st and last r.

Make 7 of these squares for back of the

yoke, and 8 for each side. Have each side of the front pointed. Place 3 squares at the bottom of each side, then 2 above. At the inner edge of each side make 3 half-squares, each of 3 leaves and ch's. Join the squares to each other by p's of the r's, as seen in the illustration. This makes a very pretty yoke for a corset-cover or chemise.

Fig. 37. Trimming for Handkerchief

The insertion is made as follows: r 3 d s, 6 p separated by 2 d s, 3 d s, close. Turn, r 5 d s, close into a half r. Turn, make another r like 1st one. Turn, 5 d s, close into a half r. Turn, 3 d s, join in last p of 1st r, 5 p separated by 2 d s, 3 d s, close. When turning the corner make 2

FIG. 35. DETAIL OF FIG. 34

extra r's on outer edge. Repeat all around the six-inch square. Sew the lace footing to outer edge of tatted insertion by 2 centre p's of r's, taking a stitch into each mesh of the footing from one r to another.

The simple tatting on outer edge of footing is made thus: r 4 d s, 7 p separated by 2 d s, 4 d s, close. Leave ¼ in. thread, 4 d s, join in last p of 1st r, 6 p separated by 2 d s, 4 d s, close. Repeat the required length. Sew to the footing by the thread between the r's, taking a stitch into each mesh of the footing and over the thread between the r's.

For this handkerchief take a six-inch square of fine linen neatly hemstitched. Sew the tatted insertion to the hem by the 2 centre p's of each r, slipping the needle between the two sides of the hem from one r to another.

FIG. 36. YOKE

FIG. 37. TRIMMING FOR HANDKERCHIEF

Fig. 38. Edge for Handkerchief

Make this edge of 2 threads, thus: r 6 d s, 5 p separated by 2 d s, 6 d s close, fasten on 2d thread and ch 4 d s, 5 p separated by 2 d s, 4 d s. Alternate r's and ch's, joining the r's to each other by the 1st p.

Sew the tatting to dotted footing an inch or inch and a half wide. Gather the border, and sew to edge of a hemstitched square.

Star for Collar

NOT ILLUSTRATED.

MATERIAL.—No. 80 thread.

These stars may be joined to form an all-over pattern, or arranged as described below, make a dainty turnover collar.

* Ring 5 d s, p, 3 d s, p, 5 d s, close, leave ⅛ in. of thread, r 6 d s, p, 6 d s, close. Repeat from * 5 times, joining the larger r's together in a circle, tie and cut.

For a collar join 6 stars in a ring by joining the 1st and 2d points of the 2d star to 2 points of the 1st; the 1st and 2d points of the 3d to the 5th and 6th of the 2d and so on. Fill the space in the centre with a star, joining the points into the p's which join stars together. Now add a star to 3 alternate sides of the hexagon, joining by 3 points and forming a triangle. Now join a star by 2 points to 2 points of a corner star in the triangle, then one by 3 points between these two, then one by 3 points between the last two. These three stars form a small triangle on one point of the large one. Let the base of the

large triangle opposite this point form the middle of the collar and join enough stars on either side, in a straight line, to make the collar as long as desired.

Edging and Insertion

NOT ILLUSTRATED.

Make a number of rosettes thus: * r 5 d s, 5 p separated by 2 d s, 5 d s, close. Repeat from * 5 times, joining by 1st and last p's, tie and cut. Chain 3 p separated by 3 d s, 2 d s, p, 3 d s; make a c l thus: r 3 d s, 3 p separated by 2 d s, 5 d s, close, r 5 d s, 5 p separated by 2 d s, 5 d s, close Repeat 1st r, ch 3 d s, join to 1st p in last ch, 2 d s, 4 p separated by 4 d s, 3 d s, join to the middle p of a r in rosette; turn work over and ch 3 d s, join to middle p of side r in c l, 5 d s, join to 1st p in middle r of c l, 3 d s, p, 3 d s, join by shuttle thread to middle p of next r in rosette, 3 d s, 4 p separated by 4 d s, 3 d s, join to next r. This forms half of a scallop. Repeat for other half, reversing work.

HEADING. Chain 2 d s, join by shuttle thread into 1st p at top, ch 2 d s, p, 2 d s, join to next p, ch, join next 2 p's together, ch, join, ch, join, ch 2 d s, 3 p separated by 4 d s, join to middle p of top r of rosette. Repeat to end. Make another row with ch's of 2 d s, p, 2 d s, between all p's

INSERTION. Join rosettes with 4-ringed figures made thus: * r 6 d s, 3 p separated by 2 d s, 6 d s, close, r 6 d s, join to 1st p in a r in a rosette, 4 d s, join to last p in next r, 5 d s, close; repeat from * joining another rosette on opposite side. Add a heading to either side.

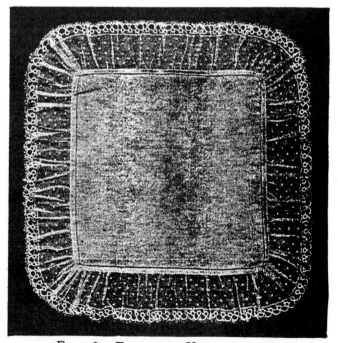

FIG. 38. EDGE FOR HANDKERCHIEF

Fig. 39. Edging

Make the pointed edge first, using shuttle and spool. Ring 4 d s, 5 p separated by 2 d s, 4 d s, close, ch 4 p separated by 2 d s, * r 4 d s, join to 1st r, 4 p separated by 2 d s, 4 d s, close, ch like last. Repeat from * 3 times; r 4 d s, join to last r, 2 d s, p, 2 d s, p, 4 d s, p, 4 d s, close, ch 5 p separated by 2 d s, r 4 d s, join to last p of last r, 4 d s, join to next p of last r, 4 d s, p, 4 d s, close, ch 5 p separated by 2 d s, r 4 d s, join to last p of last r, 4 d s, join to same p as the last r, 2 d s, p, 2 d s, p, 4 d s, close. Repeat the 1st 5 ch's and r's. This forms the border for the 1st point. For the next point make a r close to the last one, without joining, after which proceed as before until you have as many points as required.

The wheels are next made; r 8 p separated by 2 d s, close, fasten thread to 1st p, r 4 d s, 5 p separated by 2 d s, 4 d s, close; join thread to next p of centre. Repeat 7 times, joining r's by 1st and last p's, and to the point as shown in the illustration.

When all the points are filled with wheels make the upper part as follows: r 4 d s, 2 p separated by 2 d s, join to 2d p of 1st r of 1st point, 2 p separated by 2 d s, 4 d s, close. Leave ⅛ inch thread between all the r's of this border, r 4 d s, 1 p, 4 d s, close, r 4 d s, join to last large r made, 4 p separated by 2 d s, 4 d s, close, r 4 d s, join to p of small r, 4 d s, close. Make 3 more large r's with 2 small r's between joined as before, the large r's being joined to the 3 upper r's of the wheel, as seen in illustration. Proceed in this way the length required. The last row is made in the same way, joining the 2 small r's in same p with the small r's already made.

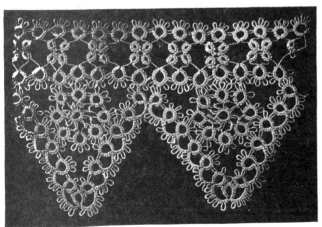

FIG. 39. EDGING

Fig. 40. Infants' Cap

MATERIALS.—No. 36 thread, one yard of No. 3 ribbon, and one and one-half yards of No. 5.

Begin in the centre of the crown with a r of 10 1 p separated by 2 d s, tie, and cut the thread. The 2d row is of 10 r's and ch's alternating, the ring of 3 p separated by 2 d s, and joined to a p of the centre; and the ch of 4 d s,

FIG. 40. INFANTS' CAP

5 p separated by 2 d s, 4 d s; 3d row is of 10 r's, same as in this row, joined to middle p of the ch and the ch's contain 9 p instead of 5.

The 4th row is formed thus: ** r 5 p separated by 2 d s, * ch 5 p separated by 2 d s, r like last, repeat from * 8 times, joining the r's by the 2d p; after making the 10th r make a ch of 9 p, joining it by middle p to ch of previous row. Repeat from ** 9 times, joining the wheels by the p's of 3 ch's as seen in illustration, fill in the spaces at the outer edge by c l's, each r of 6 d s, 5 p separated by 3 d s, 6 d s.

The next row is of 11 wheels like the one in centre of the crown, joined to each other and to ch's of previous row. These wheels reach to the neck, and the rest of the row at the neck is of 2 half wheels same as these. A half wheel is also made each side of the front at the neck to make the lower edge wide enough. Fill in spaces with c l's.

For the next row across the front make a double row of r's, each of 7 d s, 5 p separated by 3 d s, 7 d s, joined by 1st p, and one side joined to work previously done.

Make another row of 11 wheels, same as in centre of crown, with 8 ch's instead of 10, and fill in spaces with c l's or large r's.

The last row is of r's, and extends all around the cap. The outer r is same as in previous row, and is joined by 1st p. The inner r is of 3 p, not joined to each other. Make the r's close enough to make the work lie flat.

Fig. 43. Yoke

MATERIAL.—No. 50 cotton thread.

This yoke is made of two wheels, one large and one small, and joined as seen in the illustration. For the small wheel, Fig. 1, ring 5 p separated by 3 d s, close, tie on the 2d thread and ch 10 d s, p, 10 d s. Alternate the r and ch until 8 of each are made, joining the r's to each other by the 2d p.

For the large wheel, Fig. 2, make 8 r's and 8 ch's, the r's same as in the small wheel, and

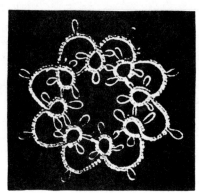

FIG. 42. SMALL WHEEL
SEE FIG. 43

the ch of 4 d s, 5 p separated by 2 d s, 4 d s, tie and cut threads. * Make a c l, each r of 5 p separated by 3 d s, r's joined to each other by 1st p. Fasten on 2d thread and ch 9 d s, turn, r 5 p separated by 2 d s, turn, ch 9 d s, join to middle p of ch of the centre wheel, ch 9 d s, turn, r 5 p separated by 2 d s, join to the 1st one by 2d p, ch 9 d s, then repeat from * 7 times.

Begin the yoke at the lower edge of the back, with three of the large wheels. The next row is 4 small wheels joined to the large ones, then 5 large wheels, then 4 small ones, then 5 large ones. This brings the yoke to the neck in the back. By the illustration the worker can readily see how the wheels are joined to form the rest of the yoke.

At the outer edge of each shoulder is a wheel somewhat different from the other 2. For this one, make a r of 6 p separated by 3 d s, tie and cut thread. Make the outer row same as the large wheel with 6 c l's instead of 8.

Medallions

NOT ILLUSTRATED.

No. 1. * Ring 9 d s, p, 9 d s, close; repeat from * 3 times, tie and cut. * Ring like others joined

FIG. 41. LARGE WHEEL. SEE FIG. 43

to a p of centre, ch 3 d s, 7 p separated by 2 d s, 3 d s, r joined to next p, ch 3 d s, 5 p separated by 2 d s, 3 d s; repeat from * 3 times joining next r in same p with last one.

No. 2. * Ring 5 d s, p, 3 d s, p, 5 d s, close, ch 12 d s; repeat from * 6 times, joining the r's together. Join both threads into top of 1st r, ch 5 p separated by 3 d s, join between next 2 scallops, repeat around wheel.

No. 3. * Ring 3 p separated by 4 d s, r 5 p separated by 4 d s; turn last r down, ch 3 p separated by 4 d s, r 4 d s, join to 2d p in large r, 4 d s, p, 4 d s, close, ch like last. Repeat from * 3 times, tie and cut.

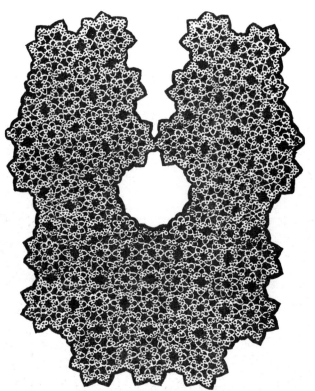

FIG. 43. TATTED YOKE. SEE FIGS. 41 AND 42

18

Fig. 44. Border

MATERIAL.—No. 36 thread.

The lace is formed of two kinds of wheels, joined in groups of 5, and the groups set together with a bar.

Make the lower wheel thus: 8 p separated by 2 d s, close and cut the thread. Around this make a row of 8 r's and ch's alternating; the r of 3 d s, p, 3 d s, join to centre, 3 d s, p, 3 d s, close. The ch of 4 d s, 7 p separated by 2 d s, 4 d s.

Make 3 of these wheels for the lower part of the section, and 2 of the 2d wheels for the upper part. The 2d wheel is formed of 8 r's and ch's alternating; the r of 5 p separated by 3 d s and joined to each other by the 2d p, the ch is the same as in the 1st wheel.

Join the wheels as seen in the illustration, and in the centre place a four-ringed figure, each r of 5 d s, 5 p separated by 2 d s, 5 d s. In the open spaces at the edge make 3 c l's, each r the same as in the centre figure. After the sections are made, join by making the bar thus: r 7 d s, 5 p separated by 3 d s, 7 d s, close, join 2d thread and ch 4 d s, 5 p separated by 2 d s, 4 d s, join to section by middle p. Repeat until 7 r's, joined by first p, and 6 ch's are made for one side. The ch at the ends has 10 p, and the other side is made like the 1st, each r being joined to the one on the opposite side. Sew the tatting to a Battenberg braid.

Fig. 45. Handkerchief Border

Begin the border by making the wheels. Ring 1 d s, 15 p separated by 2 d s, 1 d s, close, tie and cut the thread. * Ring 2 d s, p, 2 d s, join in 1st p

FIG. 44. BORDER

of r, 2 d s, p, 2 d s, close, turn, leave ¼ inch thread, r 3 p separated by 4 d s, close, turn, leave ¼ inch thread, repeat from * 14 times, joining the r's by 1st and last p's, tie and cut. Make 9 wheels for each side and join by middle p of wheels. After joining all the wheels, fitting them so as to form a square, finish the outer edge thus: Fasten 2 threads to 1st p, ch 3 d s, 5 p separated by 2 d s. 3 d s, join to p of next r, repeat 4 times, 4 d s. join to p of 2d wheel, repeat the ch all around the edge. The last row of edge is made as follows: r 8 d s, join in centre p of 1st ch in previous row, 8 d s, close, ch 3 d s, 5 p separated by 2 d s, 3 d s, r 8 d s, join in 2d p of next ch, 8 d s, **close.** Chain, r 8 d s, join in 4th p of same ch, 8 d s, **close,** repeat all around, making 2 r's, close together between the wheels.

The inside of the square is finished thus: ch 3 d s, 5 p separated by 2 d s, 3 d s, join to 2d p of wheel, repeat the ch 4 times, but do not join at the end of the 5th; instead, r 8 d s, join to last p of wheel, 8 d s, close, make a 2d r like this, close up and joining the one last made to 1st r of 2d wheel, repeat all around inside of the square, and join the border to the linen centre by centre p of three ch's of each wheel.

Edgings
NOT ILLUSTRATED.

No. 1. Chain 6 d s, p, 6 d s, r 6 d s, p, 6 d s, close, close up r 4 d s, 6 p separated by 2 d s, 4 d s, close, * ch 6 d s, p, 6 d s, join into loop between last r and ch, 6 d s, close, r 4 d s, join to 1st p in large r, 6 p separated by 2 d s, 4 d s, close. Repeat from *.

No. 2. Chain 6 d s, p, 6 d s, r 8 d s, p, 4 d s, p, 4 d s, close; close up * r 3 p separated by 4 d s and joined by 1st p to last r. Repeat from * twice, making a c l. Chain 6 d s, repeat 1st 2 r's made and 1st ch, joining the r's to c l and each other and the ch to 1st ch by 1st p; join to p of last r and repeat from beginning, joining 1st r into same p with ch and 2d to next p. Finish with a crocheted ch at top joined by a s c in each p.

FIG. 45. BORDER FOR HANDKERCHIEF

Fig. 46. Ladies' Collar

MATERIAL.—No. 60 lace thread.

The collar is formed of 6 sections, each containing 6 wheels, put together with straight bars made with 2 threads. For the wheel * r 12 p separated by 2 d s, tie, and cut the thread. Then r 3 d s, p, 3 d s, join to p, 3 d s, p, 3 d s, close, turn, leave ¼ inch of thread, r 7 d s, 7 p separated by 2 d s, 7 d s, close, turn, and make another small r. Repeat from * 11 times, joining each small r to the centre, and the large ones to each other by the first p. Make 6 wheels and join by p's, as seen in the illustration.

Fill in spaces on 2 sides by c l's, each r of 7 d s, 5 p separated by 3 d s, 7 d s, close. Make 6 of these sections and join by the bar, which has 13 r's and 12 ch's on each side. The r is the same as in the c l, and the ch of 4 d s, 7 p separated by 2 d s, 7 d s. At the ends the ch has 11 p. Join the r's to each other by the 1st p, and to the one on the opposite side by the middle p. Join the ch's to r's in the wheels and c l's.

After the sections are all joined fill in the spaces at the top with c l's, placing one each side of the end of the bars.

Across the top of the collar make a double row of r's. Each r same as in the bars, and those in each row joined to each other, and lower row joined to the collar.

Straighten the collar into shape, and press with a wet cloth over it. If the collar is desired fuller than the pattern, 2 more sections may be added, making it a perfect circle. This one is large enough to fit at the base of a stock on a medium-sized bust.

Trimming

NOT ILLUSTRATED.

This is a variation of the design seen in Fig. 61 and also in Fig. 27. It is adaptable to many purposes, as it is equally effective made with fine or coarse thread, and may be made of any width desired. The r's consist of 6 d s, p, 6 d s, close; ch's the same, except the r's at the top, which have an extra p for use in sewing the edge to band.

Ring 2 d s, p, 4 d s, p, 6 d s, close, ch 6 d s, p, 6 d s, r joined to last r, * r close up, turn, bring the spool thread up between the r's, pass it around the fingers and make a ch, r; repeat from * as many times as desired. To turn, ch, * r joined to p which joins last 2 r's, ch, r, joined to same p forming a group of 4 r's, pass shuttle under spool thread, repeat from * to end of row, making the last r of 6 d s, join, 4 d s, p, 2 d s, close. Chain 2 d s, p, 3 d s, p, 3 d s, p, 2 d s. Repeat from the beginning, joining ch's to those in last row.

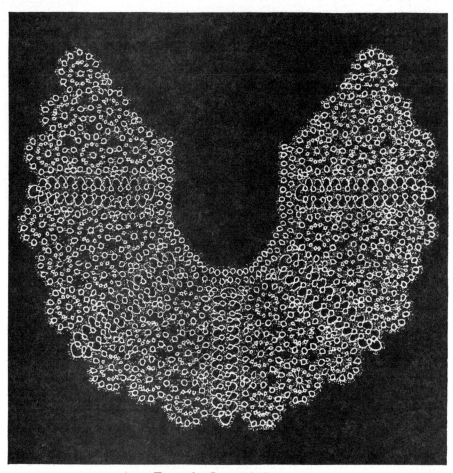

FIG. 46. LADIES' COLLAR

This design made with crochet cotton No. 50 makes a pretty collar and cuff set to wear with tailored waists, as the collar may be attached to a stiff foundation and will be found to launder well.

Another variation of this design may be made thus: r with extra p like 1st above, ch, r joined to 1st r, r close up; now turn this r over towards you so it points directly opposite the other one and the 2 threads cross between the r's; ch, r joined to last r, r close up: turn this down from you. Finish at end of row and turn same as in the design above. When the next row is finished the groups of r's and ch's will alternate and in the finished design the groups of r's run diag-

(Concluded on page 21)

Fig. 47. Collar and Cuffs

MATERIAL.—No. 80 lace thread, either cream or white.

This collar is formed of 2 kinds of wheels, clover-leaves, and the sections are set together with straight bars. There are 6 sections of wheels and 5 bars.

For the wheel which forms the outside of the sec-

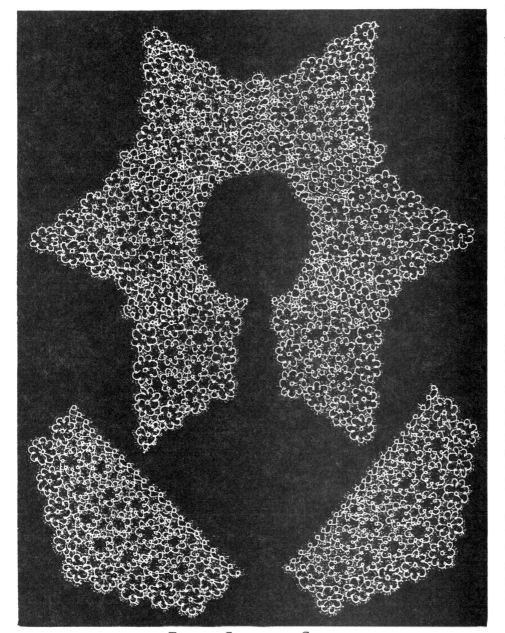

FIG. 47. COLLAR AND CUFFS

2 d s, 5 p separated by 2 d s, 2 d s, close, fasten on 2d thread, ch like the one in the 1st wheel, and alternate the r's and ch's until you have 8 of each, joining the r's to each other by the 2d p. Make 11 of the 1st and 4 of the 2d wheels for each section, joining them in making as seen in the illustration. On each side of the section make 2 small c l's, joining each r to a p of the wheels.

After making the 6 wheel sections, place them together with the bars made thus: 7 d s, 5 p separated by 3 d s, 7 d s, close, fasten 2d thread and ch 4 d s, 7 p separated by 2 d s, 4 d s. Alternate r's and ch's, until you have 9 r's and 8 ch's, joining the r's to each other by the 1st p, then at the end ch 4 d s, 9 p separated by 2 d s, 4 d s, and make the other side of the bar like the 1st, joining each r to the one on the opposite side by the 3d p. The bar is fastened to the sections by the middle p of the ch's.

Along the top of the collar make a row of small c l's in the open spaces, and for the edge make a row of r's and ch's, the r of 7 d s, 5 p separated by 3 d s, 7 d s, and the ch of 4 d s, 7 p separated by 2 d s, 4 d s, the ch's joined to the rest of the collar in making (see illustration). Each cuff is formed of 11 of the 1st kind of wheel, and 13 of the 2d, with 4 half-wheels at the top edge, all joined in making by the middle p's of the ch's, and the edge finished like the edge of the collar.

(Concluded from page 20)

onally and join at the corners. This design made with knitting silk would make a handsome design for a yoke and deep cuffs. If a pointed effect is desired it may be obtained by adding a group of r's to each successive double row until the middle is reached and then decreasing in the same manner. Made with crochet cotton as a straight edge it would be suitable for trimming pillow-cases.

tions r 8 p separated by 2 d s, close and cut the thread. Ring 2 d s, p, 2 d s, join to a p of the centre, 2 d s, p, 2 d s, close, fasten on 2d thread, ch 4 d s, 5 p separated by 2 d s, 4 d s, turn, and alternate the r's and ch's until you have 8 of each, joining each r to a p of the centre. The wheel for the inside of the sections is made thus:

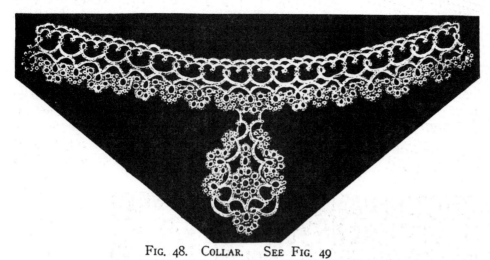

FIG. 48. COLLAR. SEE FIG. 49

Fig. 48. Collar

MATERIAL.—No. 100 thread.

Each ring and chain consists of p's separated by 2 d s. Wind shuttle and, without breaking thread from spool, commence with figure at lower edge of the collar.

1st row—Ring 19 p, close, join thread in 1st p, r 5 p, join to 3d p, * r 5 p, joining to last, join to 5th p; repeat from * 7 times. Chain 18 p, r 19 p. Work around this r 6 r's of 13 p, joining them to each other and to every 3d p in large r. Chain 18 p and repeat figures till 19 are made, joining them together as seen in the illustration of detail.

2d row—Do not break threads. Chain 5 p, r 5 p, ch 5 p, turn, r 13 p, ch 9 p, join to centre p of opposite ch, ch 9 p, r 5 p, ch 9 p, join to opposite ch as before. Continue across the collar. Tie threads firmly and cut close.

3d row—Join thread into centre p of 1st large r in 2d row. Chain 11 p, r 5 p, ch 11 p, r 5 p; join centre p to centre p of small r opposite. Continue same across the collar.

4th row—Do not break threads. Chain 11 p, join to centre p of last ch, ch 10 p, join to centre p of opposite ch, continuing across collar.

TAB.—Make wheel in centre first. Ring 19 p, work around it 7 r's of 13 p's each, tie and cut threads. Small oblong figure: Ring 5 p, leave short thread, r 13 p joining 1st p to last p in small r, r 5 p, r 19 p joining 9th and 11th p to 2 of the r's in the wheel, tie and cut threads. Now unwind some of the thread from shuttle and knot thread near the shuttle to side of figure next the centre figure of the collar. (See illustration.) Chain 5 p, join to r in centre figure of collar, ch 5 p, r 5 p, ch 18 p, r 13 p, work around it 6 r's of 5 p joining 1st r to small r on ch. Chain 9 p, join to small r of oblong figure, ch 9 p, r 19 p, work around it 6 r's of 13 p's, ch 9 p, join between r's in wheel; ch 9 p, r 19 p, work around it 9 r's of 5 p's each. Chain 9 p, join between next r's in

wheel. Chain 9 p, r 5 p, ch 9 p, join between next r's in wheel, ch 9 p, r 19 p, work around 7 r's of 13 p's each. Make other side of tab the same, joining ch's near top of tab. At the bottom of tab, join the figures with ch's; 1st ch—9 p on each side of small r; 2d ch—30 p's, tie and cut threads.

Fig. 61. Child's Cap

ILLUSTRATED ON PAGE 29

1st row—Beginning at centre of crown, * 6 d s, p, 10 d s, p, 10 d s, p, 6 d s, close. Leave ¼ in. of thread and repeat from * 7 times, joining the r's together by 1st and last p's. Tie threads and, without cutting, pass thread back of 1st r and join in its p.

2d row—* Chain 1 d s, 1 p, 2 d s, 1 p, 1 d s, join to p of next r. Repeat from * around wheel, tie and cut.

3d row—Chain 1 d s, join into 3 l p's by drawing the thread through the 1st, then the 2d and 3d, 1 d s, 8 p separated by 2 d s, 1 d s, join to next 3 l p's and repeat around wheel, tie, and cut.

4th row—Make a c l thus: * r 6 d s, p, 10 d s, p, 10 d s, p, 6 d s, close; r 6 d s, join to p of last r, 9 d s, join to last p of a group of 8 in last row, 2 d s, join to next p, 9 d s, p, 6 d s, close; repeat 1st r of c l, joining it to 2d; ch 4 l p separated by 8 d s. Repeat from * 7 times, tie and cut.

5th row—Tie thread into a l p of last row,

(*Concluded on page 24*)

FIG. 49. DETAIL OF FIG. 48

Fig. 50. Border for Handkerchief

MATERIAL.—No. 100 thread. Each ring and chain consists of picots, separated by two double stitches.

1st row—Commence with centre of the half-wheel. * Ring 23 p. Around this r, make 11 small r's of 5 p's each, joining to every other p in large r. Now ch 15 p, join to centre p of the 3d small r. Repeat 4 times, join last ch at starting point, and ch 19 p, r 5 p, ch 19 p, r 5 p, ch 5 p, r 5 p, ch 5 p, r 5 p, ch 19 p, r 5 p, ch 19 p. Repeat from * 3

first row, ch 15 p, join at corner where the 19 p ch crosses, ch 15 p, join to middle of next ch and repeat to end of row.

3d row—Tie threads to fourth p of a ch in second row, ch 9 p. Join to 12th p of ch. At corner omit 1 ch. Repeat to end of row.

4th row—Chain 9 p, join to centre p of a ch in third row. At corner join 2 chains of third row together. Repeat to end of row.

5th row—Ring 5 p, ch 6 p, join to centre p of a ch in fourth row, ch 6 p, r 5 p, ch 6 p, join to

FIG. 50. BORDER FOR HANDKERCHIEF.   SEE FIG. 51

times. After the 4th half-wheel is finished, make, instead of a small r at top of small figure, one of 23 p to form the corner half-wheel, letting the chains of 19 p overlap each other to turn corner.

Work rings of 13 picots around the 15 p chains and join to the small figures of 5 p chains and 5 p rings, as seen in the illustration. On the outer edge of each of the two half-wheels make 13 r, each of 13 p. Tie the thread in third p of first ch, join 3 r to the next ch, 5 to the next, 3 to the next, and 1 to the last, as seen in the illustration.

2d row—Tie threads into centre p of a ch in

next ch, etc. At corner skip 2 chains in fourth row.

To finish the edge of the three half-wheels of the corners, work around them chains of 19 p each, join to every other large r at centre p.

On these chains work small rings of 5 p; 4 on first ch, 5 on second, 6 on third, 5 on fourth, 3 on fifth, of the first half-wheel. On the centre half-wheel make 6 chains, with 3 r on first ch, 5 on second, 6 on third and fourth, 5 on fifth, 3 on sixth chain. Finish third half-wheel like first.

23

(Concluded from page 22)

* ch 1 d s, 4 l p separated by 2 d s, 1 d s, join to next l p; repeat from * around wheel.

6th row—Like 3d, joining into each group of 4 l p, and making 4 p separated by 2 d s between joinings.

7th row—Like 4th, making 16 c l's and joining over each alternate group of l p's in 5th row.

8th row—Like 5th, joining 1st and last p's in ch's of 7th row together, and making 4 l p separated by 2 d s, between.

9th row—Like 6th.

10th row—Like 7th, making 15 c l's with 2 clusters of l p's in 8th row between c l's and leaving 5 clusters unused at back of cap.

11th row—Like 10th only it is made free from the rest and the middle r of c l consists of 6 d s, join, 10 d s, p, 10 d s, p, 6 d s, close.

12th row—This row joins the 11th to the work. Tie thread into 1st l p of 10th row, join to 1st p of 1st ch in 11th row with spool thread, ch 1 d s, p, 2 d s, p, 1 d s, join by drawing shuttle thread through the next l p in both rows, 1 d s, 3 p separated by 2 d s, 1 d s, join to next p in both rows, 1 d s, 3 p separated by 2 d s, 1 d s, now draw thread through next 2 p's in both rows. Repeat to end of row.

13th row—Tie thread into p of middle r of 1st c l in 11th row, ch 1 d s, 12 l p, separated by 2 d s, 1 d s, join to next c l; repeat to end of row.

14th row—Tie thread into 1st 4 l p's in 13th row, ch 1 d s, 4 l p separated by 2 d s, 1 d s, join to next 4 l p's. Repeat to end of row.

15th row—Tie thread into 1st 4 l p's in 14th row, ch 1 d s, then as many p's separated by 2 d s as necessary to reach the next group and make a firm edge. Repeat to end of row.

16th row—Ring 6 d s, p, 4 d s, 7 l p separated by 2 d s, 4 d s, p, 6 d s, close; ch 2 p separated by 2 d s, join to 1st p of last row, 2 p separated by 2 d s. Repeat, joining closely enough to make a full border and continue this border across the lower edge of cap.

Doily

NOT ILLUSTRATED.

MATERIAL.—Coarse crochet cotton.

This is a very pretty border for a round doily and so simple it can easily be made without an illustration.

1st row—This is the outer row and consists of 19 rosettes joined in a circle and made thus: centre, r 5 p separated by 2 d s, close, join thread into 1st p, and * ch 5 d s; now make a c l thus: r 5 d s, 3 p separated by 2 d s, 3 d s, close, r 3 d s, join to last p of last r, 2 d s, 4 p separated

(Concluded on page 25)

FIG. 51. DETAIL OF FIG. 50. FULL SIZE

Fig. 52. Handkerchief Border

MATERIAL.—No. 60 cotton is used.

First make the wheels, beginning with a small **r** in the centre, of 12 p separated by 2 d s: around this r follows a row, consisting of small and large r's, worked alternately; the small r is made of 10 d s, join to a p of the centre r,

2d row—Tie thread into a middle p of a right-hand inner c l of a rosette, and * ch 5 d s, join to middle p of 1st c l in next rosette, 9 d s, **p,** 9 d s, join in middle p of next c !. Repeat from * around the border.

3d row—* Ring 4 d s, 2 p separated by 2 d s, join to a p in 2d row, 2 p separated by 2 d s, 4 d s, close, ch 8 d s, p, 8 d s, r 7 d s, join to last

FIG. 52. BORDER FOR HANDKERCHIEF

10 d s,—the large r of 5 d s, p, 5 d s, 3 p separated by 2 d s, 5 d s, p, 5 d s; repeat this 11 times, tie. Join wheels and r's as seen in illustration.

For the row inside the wheels, the r's consist of the same stitches as the large r's in wheels. The arrangement of the corner is clearly shown in the illustration.

(Concluded from page 24)

by 2 d s, 3 d s, close, repeat 1st r, joining to 2d, ch 5 d s, join to next p of centre r. Repeat from * 4 times, joining the c l's together by 1st and last p's. Join the 2d rosette to 1st by middle p's of a c l in each rosette. Join the 3d so as to leave one c l free at outer edge and two on inner edge of border.

p in last r, 7 d s, close. Repeat r close up, ch 8 d s, p, 8 d s. Repeat from * around border. With needle run a thread through the inner p's and draw the work smooth. Make a centre of linen to fit and whip the border on.

Medallion

NOT ILLUSTRATED.

For the centre make a four-ringed figure, each r of 9 d s, p, 9 d s, close, tie and cut. *Ring 4 d s, p, 5 d s, join to a r of central figure, 5 d s, p, 4 d s, close, ch 7 d s, p, 5 d s, p, 5 d s, p, 7 d s, r like 1st and joined to same p of centre, ch 6 d s, p, 5 d s, p, 5 d s, p, 6 d s. Repeat from * 3 times, tie and cut.

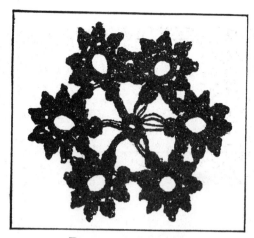

FIG. 53. MEDALLION

Fig. 53. Medallion

MATERIAL.—Black knitting silk.

Cut from cardboard a strip ⅓ of an in. wide by 1 in. long. With single thread make 2 d s; now over the cardboard * make a p, remove cardboard, make 2 d s, repeat from * 6 times, making 6 l p, 2 d s and close r.

For daisies r 9 p separated by 3 d s, close, leave short length of thread, r 4 d s, fasten to a l p, 4 d s, close, fasten by shuttle-thread to a p of large r; make and fasten in like manner the remaining 8 r's. In making the next daisy, fasten to centre as you did the first one. Make half of next r and fasten to corresponding r of first daisy.

Fig. 54. Border

Make several daisies and half daisies first. The daisy is composed of 4 large and 4 small petals, and the half daisy of 3 large and 2 small petals, made thus: LARGE PETAL.—Fifteen d s, 10 p separated by 2 d s, 15 d s, close. SMALL PETAL. —Close up, 11 d s, 10 p separated by 2 d s, 11 d s, close. When the figure is finished tie and make the SMALL SQUARE FIGURE thus: 2 d s, p, 2 d s, 1 p, 2 d s, p, 2 d s, 1 p, 2 d s, p, 2 d s, close; * 2 d s, join to last p in 1st r, 2 d s, join to l p, 2 d s, p, 2 d s, 1 p, 2 d s, p, 2 d s, close. Repeat from *, then 2 d s, join to p, 2 d s, join to l p, 2 d s, p, 2 d s, now fold the 1st r up so that it

is held between the thumb and finger, wrong side out, and, sticking the pin up through the l p from beneath, twist it half-way over from you and pull the thread through, so that this p will not be twisted when the figure is straightened; 2 d s, join to the short p in the same way, 2 d s, close, tie and cut. Now, placing this square at the left directly under the half daisy, work in the row of 5 squares (sq), working toward the right and top, joining to each other and to the daisies and half daisies as seen in the illustration. When the desired length is made, with a crochet-hook ch 3, treble crochet in centre of 1st half daisy at right, ch 10, double crochet in 2d p, ch 8, single crochet in 1st p of sq, ch 4, s c in 2d p of sq, ch 8, d c in last p but one toward centre of half daisy, ch 10, t c in centre of half daisy, and so on to the end. *2d row*—Chain 3, d c in top of t c, * ch 3, skip 3, d c; repeat from * to the end.

Medallion

NOT ILLUSTRATED.

*Ring 4 p separated by 3 d s, r 4 p separated by 4 d s, joined to last by 1st p, r like 1st, joined to last, ch 8 d s, p, 8 d s. Repeat from * 3 times, joining each ch to p of 1st, tie and cut. Tie thread to a p of a left-hand r of a c l, ** ch 2 d s, p, * 4 d s, p, repeat from * 7 times, 2 d s, join to p of 3d r in same c l, ch 2 d s, p, 2 d s, join to next r. Repeat from ** 3 times; join to 1st p of ch, ch 2 d s, p, 2 d s, join to next p; repeat 7 times, 2 d s, join to next p, 2 d s, join to next p; continue around; in last row make 2 d s, p, 2 d s, between all p's.

FIG. 54. BORDER FOR TRIMMING

Fig. 55. Insertion

Ring 5 p separated by 2½ d s, ch the same, repeat to desired length. Make another row, joining as seen in the illustration.

3d row—Chain 4 d s, p, 4 d s, join to 2d p of 2d row, repeat ch, join to 4th p of same ch, repeat to end.

4th row—* Ring 3 p separated by 4 d s, ch 4 d s, join to p of 3d row, 4 d s, repeat to end.

5th row—Make like 4th row, joining 2 r's to each ch in 1st row.

6th row—Make like 3d row, joining to each p in 5th row.

Fig. 56. Doily

MATERIAL.—No. 40 thread.

Begin in the centre with a r of 14 1 p separated by 2 d s. Around this make a double row of r's, the small one of 3 d s, 3 p separated by 3 d s, 3 d s and joined to a p of the centre, the large r of 7 d s, 7 p separated by 3 d s, 7 d s, and joined to each other by the first p.

The 2d row is formed of c l's and ch's alternating. The r of the c l is of 5 d s, 5 p separated by 2 d s, 5 d s, and the 2d r of the leaf joined to the middle p of the large r in preceding row. The ch has 4 d s, 11 p separated by 2 d s, 4 d s.

The 3d is a row of double r's. The small r same as in the centre wheel, and the large one same as in the c l. Join the large r's to each other by the 1st p, and 3 of the small r's to each ch of preceding row.

The 4th row is large and small r's same as

FIG. 55. INSERTION

last row with plain ch between. Make the small r, joining to r of last row, with 2 threads ch 10 d s, then the large r, then ch, and repeat around the doily.

The 5th row is of r's and ch's alternating. The r is like the large one of the last row, and the ch has 4 d s, 7 p separated by 2 d s, 4 d s. Make this row with the r's joined to each other and full enough to make the work lie flat.

Press the doily with a damp cloth over it.

Doily

NOT ILLUSTRATED.

MATERIAL.—Crochet cotton No. 50, and two shuttles.

This border consists of 6 sections. Commence with a four-ringed figure for the centre of a section made thus: r 3 d s, 8 p separated by 2 d s, 3 d s, close; repeat 3 times, joining r's together by 1st and last p's, tie and cut.

1st row—Make a * c l thus: r 3 d s, 5 p separated by 2 d s, 3 d s, close, r 3 d s, join to last, 3 d s, join to 1st p of a r in the central figure, 2 d s, join to 1st p of r at right of this one, 3 d s, p, 3 d s, close, r like 1st in c l, ch 5 d s, 7 p separated by 2 d s, r 6 d s, join to 2d p of right-hand r of c l, 6 d s, close, ch 4 p separated by 2 d s, r 6 d s, p, 6 d s, close, ch 7 p separated by 2 d s, 5 d s. Repeat from * 3 times, joining c l's and r's around the central figure, tie and cut.

2d row—Tie threads into 3d p of the ch of 4 p and ch 3 d s, 3 p separated by 2 d s, join to 2d p of next ch of 7 p's, ch 7 p separated by 2 d s, 4 d s. With 1st shuttle, r 4 d s, 2 p separated by 2 d s, join to the 5th p of ch of 7 p's in 1st row, 2 p separated by 2 d s, 4 d s, close; repeat r close up, joining to last by 1st p and by 3d to 3d p of next ch of 7 p in 1st row. Drop this shuttle and with the 2d one r 4 d s, join to last p of ch of 7 p's in this row, 4 p separated by 2 d s, 4 d s, close, ch 4 d s, join to r, 6 p separated by 2 d s, join to 6th p of ch of 7 p's in 2d row, ch 3 p separated by 2 d s, 4 d s. With 1st shuttle r 4 d s, 2 p separated by 2 d s, join to 2d p in ch of 4 p's in 2d row, 2 d s, join to next p, 2 p separate l·by 2 d s, 4 d s, close. With 2d shuttle * r 4 d s, join to 1st p of

(Concluded on page 28)

FIG. 56. DOILY

Fig. 57.   Dress Trimming

MATERIAL.—This trimming may be made of black or cream silk, or of white linen thread to trim a white linen dress

Begin in the centre of the wheel. Fill the shuttle, without breaking the thread, r 7 d s, 1 l p, 7 d s, close. With 2 threads ch 10 d s, * r 7 d s, join to 1 p, 7 d s, close, ch 10 d s. Repeat from * 5 times, ch 4 d s, 5 p separated by 2 d s, 4 d s, join in top of r of previous row. Repeat all around the wheel, tie and cut. Ring 7 d s, join in 2d p of ch in previous row, 7 d s, close, ch 10 d s, r, join to 4th p of same ch. Repeat until there are 14 r's and ch's. Without cutting thread ch 4 d s, 5 p separated by 2 d s, 4 d s, join in top of r of previous row. Repeat around wheel, tie, and cut the threads. Join the wheels as seen in the illustration.

Figs. 58, 59.   Trimming for Collar and Cuff

Take a piece of handkerchief linen, 2 inches wide and the required length. Draw out 10 threads all around ½ in. from the edge, and fold the hem evenly along the space drawn out. Hemstitch, taking 8 threads at a time. Turn and divide the group of 8 threads, taking 4 threads from each group and hemstitch the same as the hem. Finish the top with a band ¼ in. longer than the hemstitched linen.

Thirty c l's of the tatted edging are required for a 14-inch collar, and 22 clover-leaves for a 9-inch cuff.

The c l edging is made thus: Chain 5 d s, one very small p, 4 d s, r 3 d s, 7 p separated by 2 d s, 3 d s, close, ch 4 d s, r 3 d s, join in last p of 1st r, 8 p separated by 2 d s, 3 d s, close, ch 4 d s, r like the 1st one, ch 4 d s, join the last ch to very small p in 1st ch. Turn, ch 5 d s, 9 p separated by 2 d s, 5 d s, 1 very small p, 4 d s. Make another c l like the 1st one, joining the last ch of 4 d s to very small p. The edging is sewed to the collar by the 5 centre p's of each long ch, slipping the needle between the two sides of the hem from one ch to the

FIG. 57.   DRESS TRIMMING

next. Press on a well-padded board on a damp cloth.

(Concluded from page 27)

ch, 4 p separated by 2 d s, 4 d s, close. Repeat from * twice, joining to each other, ch 4 d s, join to r, 2 p separated by 2 d s, join to 2d p of next ch in 2d row. Make 3 more of the 3-ringed figures and 2 of those with 4 rings, and ch's at top to correspond with the other side, then ch 3 d s and

FIG. 58.   TRIMMING FOR CUFF.   SEE FIG. 57

join to p at beginning. Make 6 of these sections, joining them in a ring with a hexagonal opening in the centre. Cut a linen centre to fit and buttonhole the edge, then sew the border on.

This design may be adapted to many purposes The 4th corner may be finished like the others when it will make a complete square. Made of fine thread it would make handsome medallions for trimming a lingerie waist.

A number of these squares made with crochet cotton and joined at the corners would make a handsome sofa pillow cover if placed over blue linen, or knitting silk and blue china silk might be used.

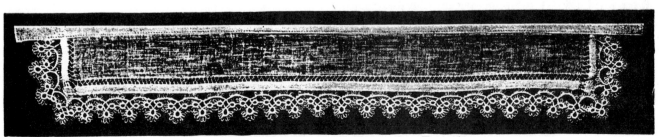

FIG. 59.   TRIMMING FOR COLLAR.   SEE FIG. 56

Fig. 60. Dress Trimming

First, for the centre, r 4 p separated by 3 d s, close, tie, and cut.

Ring 2 d s, * p, 2 d s, repeat from * 6 times or till there are 7 p, close. Chain 6 d s, * r as above, ch 6 d s, p, 6 d s, repeat from * twice, join to small centre r, ** ch 6 d s, p, 6 d s, r, repeat twice, * ch 6 d s, r, repeat once, * ch 6 d s, join to 1st p in preceding ch, 6 d s, r, repeat once, six d s, join to next ch, 6 d s, join to centre r. Now repeat from ** twice and half again, joining last short ch of 6 d s to the 1st r made and cut. This forms a 4-pointed star.

Each corner contains 3 4-ringed figures made and arranged as follows: r 6 p separated by 3 d s, close, repeat r, close up, joining to 1st r; repeat r again, joining to 2d r, and also by middle p, to middle p of the 2d r made in the star; repeat r again, joining to 3d r and to 3d r in star and by last p to 1st r, sticking the pin through this p from beneath and twisting it half over from you to pull the thread through, so that the p shall not be twisted when the work is finished; tie and cut. Now make a similar figure, joining it by the 2 middle p's of the 2d r to the 2 middle p's of the 1st r in the 1st figure and by the 3d and 4th r's to the corresponding r's in the 2d point of star.

For the 3d figure which fills the corner make the 1st and 2d r's like the others, joining the 2d r by the 5th p to the 2d p in the 2d r of the 1st

FIG. 60. DRESS TRIMMING

figure: for the 3d r, 3 d s, join to 2d r, 2 d s, join to free p of 1st r in 1st figure, 2 d s, join to free p of 2d r of 2d figure, 2 d s, p, 3 d s, close. Fourth r like 1st and 2d, joining by 2d p to 5th p in 1st r of 2d figure. Now make the large r to fill open space. One d s, join to middle p of 1st r in 2d point of star, 10 d s, join to free p in 2d r in 2d figure, 3 d s, join to next free p, 10 d s, join to middle p of last r in 1st point of star, 1 d s, close tie and cut. Fill in the other 3 corners in the same manner.

Child's Cap
NOT ILLUSTRATED

As more than one spool of knitting silk is required for this cap, it is best to purchase 2 and reserve one for filling the shuttle so that the spool thread need not be cut except at the end of rows. When necessary to join the silk always do so close up to a ring or the end of a chain and then work 3 or 4 stitches over the ends, when they may be cut close and the knot will be invisible and will not pull out.

First make the wheel in centre of crown thus: Ring 2 p separated by 2 d s, close; leave ⅛ in. of thread, r 3 p separated by 5 d s, close; leave ⅛ in. of thread, make another small r like the 1st and join by the 1st p to 2d p of 1st small r; leave ⅛ in. of thread, make another large r, joining by the 1st p to the 1st large r; continue till there are 12 small and 12 large r's joined in a wheel, tie and cut.

In the rest of these directions, unless otherwise stated. a r consists of 6 d s, p, 6 d s, and a ch of the same.

1st row around wheel—Make a ch, joining by its p to a p of one of the large r's in wheel; 2 r's close together; * pass shuttle under spool

FIG. 61. CHILD'S CAP. SEE PAGE 22

thread toward you and make a ch, joining to the next r in wheel; then 2 more r's, joining the 1st one to the 2d one of the 1st group. Repeat from star around the wheel, tie and cut.

2d row—* Make a r, join it to a p which joins 2 r's in the 1st row; ch, another r joined to same p, ch. Repeat from star around wheel, tie and cut.

3d row—Like 1st. *4th row*—Like 2d, except that there are only 3 r's in each alternate group. When this row is complete do not cut.

5th row—Chain 6 d s, join to p of 1st ch to right, ch 6 d s, r, ch, joining to next ch in 4th row; continue like 1st row around to within 1 ch of the commencing point where you tie and cut.

6th row—Counting toward right of centre tie thread into p joining 2d group of r's, ch 6 d s, working the ends in, r, joining to p which joins the next group; ch, r, joining to same p, pass shuttle under spool thread toward you and make another r close up, joining it to the next group and repeat till you reach the 2d group of r's at left of centre, tie and cut.

7th row—Make a r, joining to 1st p in 6th row, ch, * r, joining to next p, repeat to end of row. Do not cut, but twisting the two threads leave ½ in.

8th row—Like 1st row; at the end leave ½ in. of twisted threads.

9th row—Like 6th row. *10th row*—Like 7th row except that it is reversed, being joined to the 9th by ch's instead of r's; at the end pass both threads behind the r and join to p.

11th row—Chain 6 d s, and continue like 8th row; at end leave ½ in. of twisted threads and join to p of 1st r.

12th row—Chain 6 d s, continue like 9th row. When this row is finished continue across the bottom, making ch's and joining at the end of each row. A silk lining and ties may be added.

Fig. 62. Medallion

The points of the star are made 1st thus: r 4 d s, 5 p separated by 2 d s, 4 d s, close, * ch 5 p separated by 2 d s, r like 1st, joining by 1st p to last p of 1st r. Repeat from star twice. Chain 8 p separated by 2 d s, r, joined by 3d p to 3d p of last r, * ch 5 p separated by 2 d s, r, joined by 1st p to last p in preceding r and by 3d p to 3d p of the 3d r made. Repeat from star twice. Chain 4 d s. This finishes one point. Repeat 7 times, joining 3d p in 1st ch to 3d p in last ch of 1st point. Join to 1st point, turn, * ch 4 d s, p, 4 d s, join to 1st p in r, ch 4 d s, p, 4 d s, join to last p in next r. Repeat from star 7 times, tie and cut thread. For the centre, r 8 p separated by 2 d s, leave one-

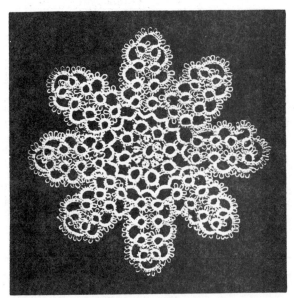

FIG. 62. MEDALLION

eighth inch thread, * r 4 d s, p, 4 d s, join to a p in last row of star, 4 d s. join to next p, 4 d s, p, 4 d s, close. Leaving very short thread, r 2 d s, join to 1st p in large centre r, 2 d s, close. Repeat from star 7 times, joining each large r to the preceding one.

Trimming
NOT ILLUSTRATED.

This trimming is worked back and forth without cutting the thread and is suitable for a handkerchief or centrepiece border, as a square corner may be formed.

The work is commenced at a corner thus: r 5 d s, p, 5 d s, close, ch 5 d s, p, 5 d s, r 3 d s, 7 p separated by 2 d s, 3 d s, close, ch 6 d s, r like last, ch 6 d s, * r 3 d s, 3 p separated by 2 d s, 3 d s, p, 3 d s, 3 p separated by 2 d s, 3 d s, close, ch 5 d s, join in p of 1st ch made, 5 d s. Repeat from * joining r to last by 2d p and ch

(Concluded on page 31)

.FIG. 63. DETAIL OF FIG. 64

Fig. 64. Waist Set

MATERIALS.—Silk, silkateen or mercerized cotton.

Make the oblong medallion in the centre first, thus: * r 4 d s, 5 p, separated by 2 d s, 4 d s, close, r 4 d s, join to last p of 1st r, 15 p separated by 2 d s, 4 d s, close. Repeat from *, tie and cut.

Join thread to the left-hand picot of small r, r 14 p separated by 2 d s, 15 d s, close, fasten to middle p of same r, 15 d s, join to p of last r, 11 p separated by 2 d s, 15 d s, draw up, join to last or 3d p, r 15 d s, join to last p of middle r, 14 p separated by 2 d s, close, and fasten to the 3d p again, tie and cut thread. This finishes one fan. Work a fan like this on the other small r.

* Ring 4 d s, p, 2 d s, p, 2 d s, join to 5th p of one of the large r's in oblong medallion, 2 d s, p, 2 d s, p, 4 d s, close, repeat close up, joining to 5th p on the other side of large r; this will give you 2 small r's at the end of large r, in medallion. Now without cutting the thread make another fan like that on the small r's, joining each r at the bottom of the small ones. Tie and cut thread. This makes one section.

Make the required number of sections and join them thus: tie the thread to 5th p of remaining large r in medallion, 4 d s, p, 2 d s, p, 2 d s, join to 3d p of middle long r in the second fan in next section, 2 d s, p, 2 d s, p, 4 d s, close, join to middle p of medallion. Make another r like this, joining at proper places, tie thread and cut.

COLLAR.—Take one large section with the three fans, make 2 more with the fans on the two small r's and 2 more half ones. Join them with 4 small r's between instead of 2. For this **set,** there are 5 strips. The 1st has 5 sections with the collar attached to the top one, 4 sections, joined for each side, and 4 for each cuff.

(Concluded from page 30)

to p of 1st r made. Ring like last and joined to it, tie and to avoid knots unwind and cut off a yard or so of thread from both shuttle and spool, to be used later in finishing this corner. Now r 5 d s, p, 5 d s, * ch 5 d s, p, 5 d s, join by shuttle thread to middle p of last large r made. Repeat from * twice, ch 6 d s, r 3 d s, 7 p separated by 2 d s, 3 d s, close, ch 6 d s, * r 3 d s, 3 p separated by 2 d s, 3 d s, p, 3 d s, 3 p separated by 2 d s, 3 d s, close, ch 5 d s, join to p of 1st ch in last row. Repeat from * twice joining the r's together and ch's to those in last row, r like others, ch 5 d s, join to p of 1st r in last row, 5 d s, 5 p separated by 2 d s, 5 d s, p, 5 d s, join to middle p of large r. Continue making 4 r's and ch's in each row, till as long as desired for side of square. When the next corner is reached, having completed a row of ch's, make the next row with only 3 r's and ch's, then r 6 d s, join to p of next ch in last row, 6 d s, close and cut threads an inch long. Now tie threads into middle p of the last r in last row and, working down ch 5 d s, p, 5 d s, join to next r; finish this row like the rest and returning make only 1 r and ch, then r 5 d s, join to p of next ch, 5 d s, close. This completes half of the corner; now ch 5 d s, p, 5 d s, r joined by 3d p to 3d p of last r made, ch 6 d s, r like others at end of rows, ch 6 d s, large r, ch joined to p of ch in last row, r ch joined to p of small r, then a large r joined by last p to corresponding p in large r, tie the threads to loose ends and cut.

To commence the next side, tie the threads into the r of 12 d s above and make the row of 3 ch's to correspond with the row which ended with the r of 12 d s. When making the ch at the top of the next row, join by 1st 2 p's of group of 5 to the corresponding ones in 1st half of corner. By looking at this corner you will see how to form the last one. When the place is reached where the long threads were left, wind one on the shuttle and finish the corner with them. To complete the corners tie threads into the middle p of the left-hand one of the 2 r's which are joined and ch 5 d s, r like others, ch 5 d s, tie into middle p of 2 d r, and cut.

This design may be made wider or narrower as desired, and adapted to many purposes. One or more rows of the rings and chains, worked lengthwise, would make a suitable insertion to go with it.

FIG. 64. WAIST SET. SEE FIG. 63

Fig. 65. Doily

Take a round piece of linen the size desired for centre of the doily, fold a narrow hem and hem neatly. Fill the shuttle with No. 30 thread. Without breaking from the spool join the thread to the linen by piercing a hole into the hem with a large pin or needle and draw the thread through with a crochet needle, then slip the shuttle through the loop and draw up.

3d row—Chain 3 d s, 5 p separated by 2 d s, 3 d s, join to centre p of r in previous row. Repeat all around.

The wheels are made thus: r 1 d s, 9 l p separated by 2 d s, 1 d s, close, tie and cut thread. Chain 3 d s, 5 p separated by 2 d s, 3 d s, join to 1st l p. Repeat 8 times, tie and cut thread.

Ring 8 d s, join in 2d p of ch in previous row, 8 d s, close, ch 3 d s, 5 p separated by 2 d s, 3 d s, r like 1st one, join in 4th p of ch in previous

FIG. 65. DOILY

Chain 4 d s, 5 p separated by 2 d s, 4 d s, join to the linen with crochet needle ⅓ in. from the 1st joining. Repeat the ch all around. Tie and cut thread.

2d row—Ring 3 d s, p, 3 d s, join to 2d p of ch in previous row, 3 d s, p, 3 d s, close. Turn, leave ¼ in, r 3 d s, 7 p separated by 2 d s, 3 d s, close. Turn, leave ¼ in. thread, 3 d s, join in last p of 1st r, 3 d s, join in 4th p of ch, 3 d s, p, 3 d s, close. Turn, make another r of 7 p. Repeat all around.

row. Repeat all around. Join the wheels to each other and to the doily by the centre p's of last ch.

Edgings
NOT ILLUSTRATED.

No. 1. * Ring 3 p separated by 3 d s, leave short length of thread, r 5 d s, p, 5 d s, close; leave same length of thread; repeat from * joining the

(Concluded on page 33)

FIG. 66. MALTESE MEDALLIONS

Fig. 66. Maltese Medallions

For 1st wheel make a * ring of 5 p's separated by 2½ d s, close and attach 2d thread. Chain 2 p separated by 2½ d s. Repeat from star 23 times, joining 3d r by 2d p to 4th p of 1st r. Join last ch to top of 1st r, tie and cut. Join wheels as seen in illustration.

For square in centre of Maltese cross put single thread through a p of wheel and tie closely and firmly the 2d thread. Chain 12 d s, join to 2d wheel by centre p of 3d r, ch 12 d s, join to 3d wheel and so on until square is complete.

Fig. 67. Trimming for Tie

MATERIAL.—No. 70 thread.

* For the c l at top make the r's of 5 d s, 6 p separated by 3 d s, 5 d s, close. Close up, r 5 d s, join to last p, 5 p separated by 3 d s, 5 d s, close. Repeat 1st r, joining to 2d. Join by 1st p and last.

Chain 6 d s, p, 6 d s, 3 p separated by 3 d s, 6 d s, 1 small p, 6 d s, join to centre p of last side r, 6 d s, 1 small p, 6 d s; r 6 d s, join to 6th p of middle r, 6 d s, close; ch 6 d s, then a c l as directed; when this is finished make a ch of 6 d s, r 6 d s, p, 6 d s, close; ch 6 d s, join to p, 6 d s, p, 6 d s, join; 6 d s, 3 p separated by 3 d s, 6 d s, p, 6 d s, repeat from *. The tie has a hem and 2 tucks, hemstitched above the tatting.

(Concluded from page 32)

large r's together by 1st and last p's but leaving the small ones free.

No. 2. Ring 5 p separated by 3 d s, close up, r like last; turn over and down, ch 5 p separated by 3 d s and joined by 1st p to last p in 1st r made, r joined by 2d p to 4th p in 2d r made, close up, r joined by 1st p to last p in ch, ch joined by 1st p to last p in 3d r made; repeat from beginning, joining r's and ch's according to those already made. The r's will form a zig-zag line and the ch's alternate on opposite sides.

No. 3. * Ring 3 p separated by 3 d s, close, leave ¼ in., r, 5 d s, p, 3 d s, 5 p separated by 2 d s, 3 d s, p, 5 d s, close, leave ¼ in., r like 1st and joined to it, leave ¼ in., r 3 d s, join to 1st p on large r, 2 d s, p, 2 d s, p, 3 d s, close, leave ¼ in. Repeat from * as many times as desired. To form an edge to sew to garment, join thread into 1st p, draw smooth, join to next p and so on.

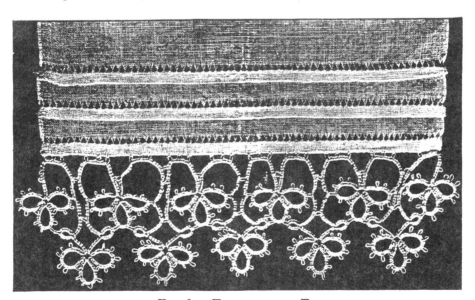

FIG. 67. TRIMMING FOR TIE

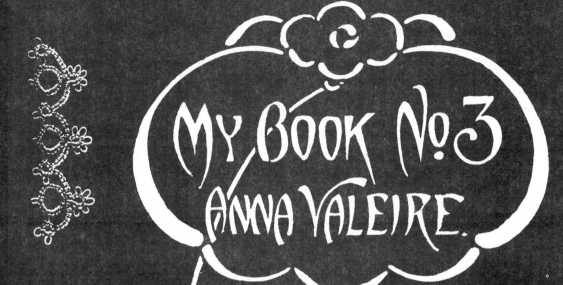

MY BOOK № 3
ANNA VALEIRE.

TATTING CRAFT

A REAL SAMPLER

OVER 100 DESIGNS

Tatting motifs are, in a way, limited, and it is with the utmost care that I have made the selection contained in this issue.

It is my idea to present the variations of even the most simple designs to afford the worker a "SAMPLER" as it is called. Thus you have shown in actual size and preserved from soiling, a collection that cannot be misplaced or lost, and a permanent record of the instructions on just these simple pieces that you would each time stop to count or create to prove them, without this instruction record. Even the most expert has wanted for ONE book containing this assortment of the simple loop. It affords an immediate review of so many variations that one is able to judge before engaging in the work, rather than regretting after that she did not use this one instead that.

The same is true of the clover leaf variations.

Another feature so much desired is the ability to follow the instructions and compare the work as it goes—this with the printed instructions immediately beside each piece is obtained here.

The size and style of type is so often a handicap to the worker, and in endeavoring to follow the thread—white on black—and the typing—black on white—how often have you felt your eyes tire?

Some books carry the instructions as first shuttle and second shuttle—but of course the second shuttle is unnecessarily wound—it might as well be called the ball thread. Others call it shuttle and second thread. Others simply call it: Ring for one thread and Chain for the other. I believe the latter is without doubt the most acceptable style, the shuttle thread being understood to be the thread for all RINGS, and the ball thread for all CHAINS. This not only simplifies the reading, but becomes automatic for the worker.

I have not limited myself to my own selection of pieces, but have sought the desires of many new and many experienced workers as to what is most wanted.

With these illustrations and simplified instructions, it is possible for any one to understand the art of tatting and carry through any of the pieces shown in this book.

No. A. Take end of thread between the thumb and first finger, then around—(I will call it the "Ring Thread") three fingers and clasp with the end. The thread now leads over to the shuttle as shown. Note how it is over the third finger of right hand, and manner of holding the shuttle.

No. B. Raise the right hand, thus extending thread above the "ring thread."

No. Ba. Preparation for next move.

No. C. Insert shuttle in front of and under the upper part of the "ring thread" as shown. Take the shuttle up thro triangle thus formed, as indicated by arrow.

No. D. Note 3rd finger of right hand is "over" thread. In this position hold this thread firm and straight—(This is the secret of success or failure, as the "ring thread" must make the stitch). Note the "ring thread" makes the loop, now raising the 2nd and 3rd fingers of left hand this loop, or knot, or stitch, is drawn down to the point of clasping. . . . . REMEMBER the "ring thread" MUST make the stitch and the shuttle thread MUST be held firm and straight from the point of clasping so it does not form a knot, as it must be drawn thro later.

No. E. Shows the stitch "drawn down." It is shown enlarged (5 doubles have been made, to show the effect—In the work these stitches would be between the thumb and finger, instead of away from the point of clasping)—draw this down till it forms the same stitch as the enlargement shows. The motion of the fingers of left hand is indicated by the finger tip shown, this motion is assisted by dropping the right hand but ALWAYS keep the shuttle thread firm and straight-taut.

Motif for flower on front cover.
Center rings—4d. p. 5d. p. 3d. p. 2d. p. 3d. p. 5d. p. 4d. close. Repeat five times joining first to last picots. Second row. Make ring. 2d. p. 2d. join to 4th picot of large ring. 2d. p. 2d. close. Leave ¼ inch thread and ring. 5d. p. 5d. p. 2d. p. 2d. p. 5d. p. 5d. close. Leave ¼ inch thread and ring. 2d. join to 3rd picot of small ring. 2d. p. 2d. p. 2d. close. Every 4th small ring joins to center medallion by center picot in large rings. The outer large rings join first to last picots

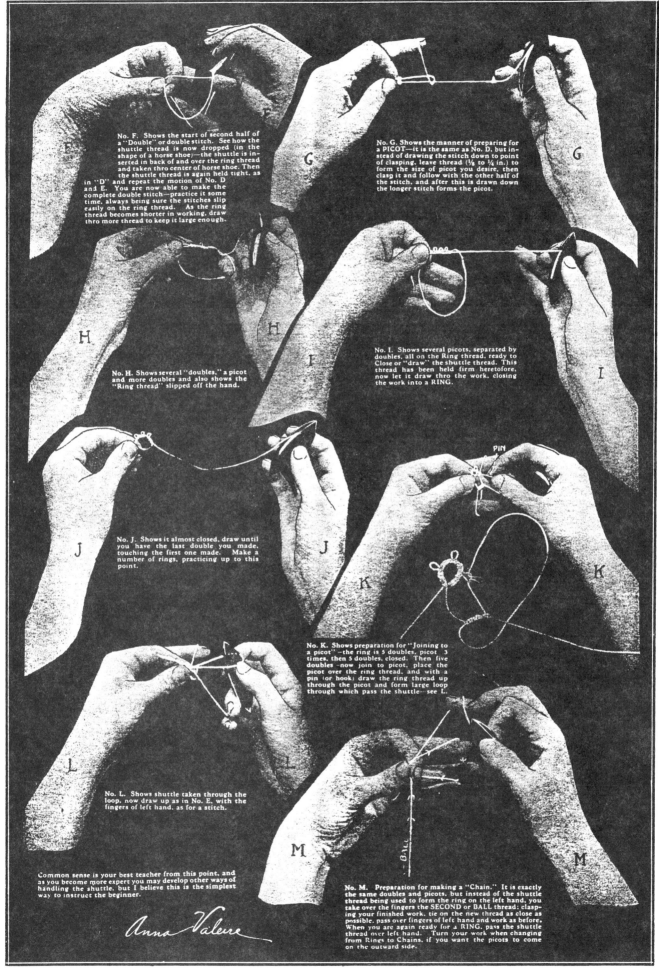

No. F. Shows the start of second half of a "Double" or double stitch. See how the shuttle thread is now dropped (in the shape of a horse shoe)—the shuttle is inserted in back of and over the ring thread and taken thro center of horse shoe. Then the shuttle thread is again held tight, as in "D" and repeat the motion of No. D and E. You are now able to make the complete double stitch—practice it some time, always being sure the stitches slip easily on the ring thread. As the ring thread becomes shorter in working, draw thro more thread to keep it large enough.

No. G. Shows the manner of preparing for a PICOT—it is the same as No. D, but instead of drawing the stitch down to point of clasping, leave thread (⅛ to ¼ in.) to form the size of picot you desire, then clasp it and follow with the other half of the stitch, and after this is drawn down the longer stitch forms the picot.

No. H. Shows several "doubles," a picot and more doubles and also shows the "Ring thread" slipped off the hand.

No. I. Shows several picots, separated by doubles, all on the Ring thread, ready to Close or "draw" the shuttle thread. This thread has been held firm heretofore, now let it draw thro the work, closing the work into a RING.

No. J. Shows it almost closed, draw until you have the last double you made, touching the first one made. Make a number of rings, practicing up to this point.

No. K. Shows preparation for "Joining to a picot"—the ring is 5 doubles, picot 3 times, then 5 doubles, closed. Then five doubles—now join to picot, place the picot over the ring thread, and with a pin (or hook) draw the ring thread up through the picot and form large loop through which pass the shuttle—see L.

No. L. Shows shuttle taken through the loop, now draw up as in No. E, with the fingers of left hand, as for a stitch.

Common sense is your best teacher from this point, and as you become more expert you may develop other ways of handling the shuttle, but I believe this is the simplest way to instruct the beginner.

Anna Valere

No. M. Preparation for making a "Chain." It is exactly the same doubles and picots, but instead of the shuttle thread being used to form the ring on the left hand, you take over the fingers the SECOND or BALL thread; clasping your finished work, tie on the new thread as close as possible, pass over fingers of left hand and work as before. When you are again ready for a RING, pass the shuttle thread over left hand. Turn your work when changing from Rings to Chains, if you want the picots to come on the outward side.

37

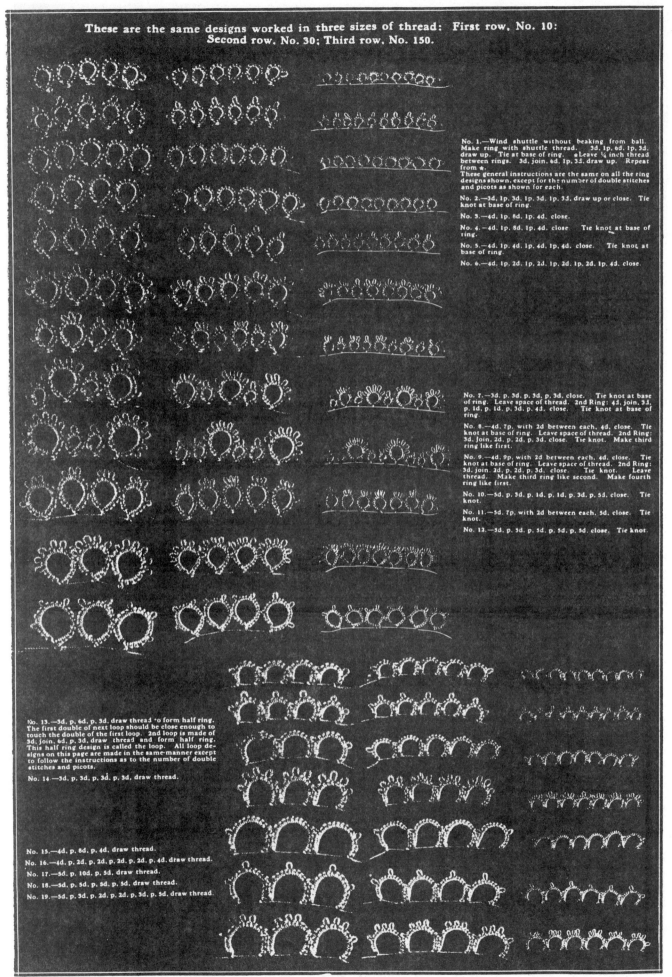

These are the same designs worked in three sizes of thread: First row, No. 10; Second row, No. 30; Third row, No. 150.

No. 1.—Wind shuttle without beaking from ball. Make ring with shuttle thread. 3d, 1p, 6d, 1p, 3d, draw up. Tie at base of ring. ★Leave ¼ inch thread between rings. 3d, join, 6d, 1p, 3d, draw up. Repeat from ★.
These general instructions are the same on all the ring designs shown, except for the number of double stitches and picots as shown for each.

No. 2.—3d, 1p, 3d, 1p, 3d, 1p, 3d, draw up or close. Tie knot at base of ring.

No. 3.—4d, 1p, 8d, 1p, 4d, close.

No. 4.—4d, 1p, 8d, 1p, 4d, close. Tie knot at base of ring.

No. 5.—4d, 1p, 4d, 1p, 4d, 1p, 4d, close. Tie knot at base of ring.

No. 6.—4d, 1p, 2d, 1p, 2d, 1p, 2d, 1p, 4d, close.

No. 7.—3d, p, 3d, p, 3d, p, 3d, close. Tie knot at base of ring. Leave space of thread. 2nd Ring: 4d, join, 3d, p, 1d, p, 1d, p, 3d, p, 4d, close. Tie knot at base of ring.

No. 8.—4d, 7p, with 2d between each, 4d, close. Tie knot at base of ring. Leave space of thread. 2nd Ring: 3d, Join, 2d, p, 2d, p, 3d, close. Tie knot. Make third ring like first.

No. 9.—4d, 9p, with 2d between each, 4d, close. Tie knot at base of ring. Leave space of thread. 2nd Ring: 3d, join, 2d, p, 2d, p, 3d, close. Tie knot. Leave thread. Make third ring like second. Make fourth ring like first.

No. 10.—5d, p, 3d, p, 1d, p, 1d, p, 3d, p, 5d, close. Tie knot.

No. 11.—5d, 7p, with 2d between each, 5d, close. Tie knot.

No. 12.—5d, p, 5d, p, 5d, p, 5d, p, 5d, close. Tie knot.

No. 13.—5d, p, 6d, p, 5d, draw thread to form half ring. The first double of next loop should be close enough to touch the double of the first loop. 2nd loop is made of 5d, join, 6d, p, 5d, draw thread and form half ring. This half ring design is called the loop. All loop designs on this page are made in the same manner except to follow the instructions as to the number of double stitches and picots.

No. 14.—3d, p, 3d, p, 3d, p, 3d, draw thread.

No. 15.—4d, p, 8d, p, 4d, draw thread.

No. 16.—4d, p, 2d, p, 2d, p, 2d, p, 4d, draw thread.

No. 17.—5d, p, 10d, p, 5d, draw thread.

No. 18.—5d, p, 5d, p, 5d, p, 5d, draw thread.

No. 19.—5d, p, 5d, p, 2d, p, 2d, p, 5d, p, 5d, draw thread.

All pieces shown on this page are a number 30 thread unless otherwise noted. Instructions for making rings always means using the shuttle thread and making chains means using the ball thread.

No. 20.—Ring. 3d, p, 3d, p, 3d, p, 3d, close. Tie on second thread. Turn. Chain 3d, p, 3d. Turn. Ring 3d, join to first ring, 3d, p, 3d, p, 3d, close.

No. 21.—Ring, 3d, p, 3d, p, 3d, p, 3d, close. Tie on second thread. Turn. Chain 3d. Ring 3d, p, 3d, p, 3d, p, 3d, close. Turn. Chain 3d. Turn. Ring 3d, join to first ring, 3d, p, 3d, p, 3d, close.

No. 22.—Ring 4d, p, 4d, p, 4d, p, 4d, close. Tie on second thread. Turn. Chain 4d, p, 4d, Turn. Ring 4d, join to first ring, 4d, p 4d, p, 4d, close.

No. 23.—Ring 4d, p, 4d, p, 4d, p, 4d, close. Tie on second thread. Turn. Chain 4d. Ring 4d, p, 4d, p, 4d, p, 4d, close. Turn. Chain 4d. Turn. Ring 4d, join to first ring, 4d, p, 4d, p, 4d, close.

No. 24.—Ring 4d, p, 3d, p, 2d, p, 2d, p, 3d, p, 4d, close. Turn. Make second ring the same. Tie on second thread. Turn. Chain 6d. Turn, make ring, 4d, connect to last picot of preceding ring and repeat rings.

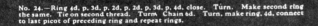

No. 25.—Make ring, 4d, p, 3d, p, 2d, p, 2d, p, 3d, p, 4d, close. Turn. Leave ¼ inch thread and make second ring. Turn. Repeat.

No. 26.—Ring 3d, p, 3d, p, 3d, p, 3d, close. Turn. Leave short thread. Make large ring, 4d, 9p with 2d between each, 4d, close. Turn. Ring 3d, join to first small ring, 3d, p, 3d, p, 3d, close. Turn. Ring 3d, join to large ring, 2d, p, 2d, p, 3d, close.

No. 27.—Ring 3d, p, 3d, p, 3d, p, 3d, close. Tie on second thread. Turn. Chain 12d. Turn. Ring 3d, p, 3d, p, 3d, p, 3d, close. Chain 12d. Make second row like first, joining middle picots of rings.

No. 28.—First ring of clover leaf: 8d, p, 6d, p, 2d, close. Second Ring: 2d, join to first ring, 6d, p, 6d, p, 2d, close. Third Ring: 2d, join, 6d, p, 6d, p, 2d, close. Tie on second thread. Turn. Make chain, 4d, p, 2d, p, 4d, join to center picot of last ring of clover leaf, 4d, p, 2d, p, 4d. With shuttle make clover leaf, joining center picot of first ring to center picot of last ring of clover leaf. Make second row of clover leaves joining center ring of cloverleaf in one row between clovers of other row.

No. 29.—Make ring, 7d, p, 14d, p, 7d, close. Tie on second thread. Turn. Chain 7d, p, 7d. Make second ring, joining first picot; then continue. Second Row: tie thread in center of ring. Chain 7d, p, 7d, join to center of next ring, and continue.

No. 30.—Make ring, 3d. p. 3d. p. 3d. p. 3d. close. Tie on second thread. Turn. Chain 2d. p. 2d. p. 2d. p. 2d. Turn. Repeat first ring; joining first picot to last picot. Second Row: Tie on thread. Chain 2. join to picot and repeat joining to base of each ring.

No. 31.—Make Ring. 5d. p. then 6p separated by 2d. 5d. close. Leave short space of thread. Make ring of 7d. join to last picot of large ring, 7d. close. Tie on second thread. Turn. Chain 5d. p. 5d. Make large ring like first, 5d. join to picot as shown.

No. 32.—First Row: Ring 4d. long picot, 4d. long picot, three times, 4d. close. Leave one inch space, repeat any desired length. Second Row: Tie thread in center of space between ring, chain, 2d. join to first picot, 6d. join to next picot, 8d. join to next, 6d. join to next, 2d. join to center of next space; repeat from start of this row. Forms a very serviceable edging for lingerie.

No. 33.—Make ring, 8d. p. 6d. p. 2d. close. Second Ring: 2d. join to first picot, 6d. p. 6d. p. 2d. close. Third Ring: 2d. join to second ring, 6d. p. 6d. p. 2d. close. Tie on second thread. Turn. Chain 10d. fasten thread in middle of last ring of clover leaf. Chain 10d. Turn and make first ring of second clover leaf, fastening to center picot of preceding ring.

No. 34.—Make ring, 8d. p. 6d. p. 2d. close. Second Ring: 2d. join to last picot, 6d. p. 6d. p. 2d. close. Third Ring: 2d. join to second ring, 6d. p. 8d. close. Tie on second thread. Chain 10d. fasten to center picot of last ring. Make small ring, 6d. p. 6d. close. Chain 10d. Turn and make first ring of second clover leaf fastening to center picot of preceding ring.

No. 35.—Make ring, 6d. p. 2d. 4p with 3d between each, 7d. close. Second Ring: 7d join to picot of first ring.—3d. 4p with 3d between each.—7d. close. Third Ring: 7d join to second ring, 3d. 3p with 3d between each, 2d. p. 6d. close. Tie and cut thread or leave ⅜ inch thread. Make next clover joining third picot of first ring to third picot of preceding ring.

No. 36.—Make ring, 5d. p. 5d. p. 5d. p. 5d. close. Second Ring: same, joining to last picot made. Third Ring: the same. Tie on second thread. Turn. Chain 5d. p. 5d. p. 5d. p. 5d. Make first ring of second clover joining to center picot of previous ring.

No. 37.—Make ring, 5d. p. 6d. p. 6d. p. 5d. close. Second Ring, same joining to last picot made. Third Ring: Same. Tie on second thread. Turn. Chain 8d. p. 3d. p. 3d. p. 8d. Turn. Ring, 5d. p. 3d. join to center picot of last clover leaf, 3d. p. 3d. p. 3d. p. 5d. close. Make another ring the same, join to last picot of ring just made. 3d. then ⚬ with 3d between each, 5d. close. Chain as before. Make clover leaf joining center of first ring to adjoining picot of ring before.

No. 38.—Make Ring, 8d. p. 8d. close. Tie on second thread. Turn. Chain 12d. Turn. Make clover leaf. Ring 8d. join to picot of small ring, 8d. close. Second Ring: 8d. p. 8d. close. Third Ring. Same. Now make chain of 12d and repeat, joining center of small ring to picot of clover as shown. Second Row: Fasten thread at base of single ring. Chain 2d. then 6p. 3d between each, 2d. join at base of next single ring.

No. 39.—Make Ring, 2d. 7p with 2d between each, 2d. close. Second ring: 2d. join to last picot of first ring, 2d. 8p with 2d between each, 2d. close. Third Ring: 2d. join to last picot of second ring, 2d. 6p with 2d between each, 2d. close. Tie on second thread. Turn. Chain 2d. 11p with 2d between each, 2d. Repeat, joining clovers as shown in center picots.

40

No. 40.—Tie two threads together, chain 4d. Make ring, 5d, 5p with 3d between each, 3d, close. Turn. Chain 4d. Turn. Ring, 3d join to last picot, 5d, 3p with 3d between each, 5d, 1p, 3d, close. Turn. Chain 4d. Turn. Make third ring like first. Turn. Chain 4d, join to start of first chain, 5d, then 6p with 3d between each, 5d, small picot, 4d. Repeat from start joining small picots of chains.

No. 41.—Tie two threads together. Chain 5d, small picot, 4d. Turn. Make ring, 5d, then 7p with 2d between each, 5d, close. Turn. Chain, 4d. Turn. Ring, 5d, join to last picot, then 8p with 2d between each, 5d, close. Turn. Chain, 4d. Turn. Ring, same, as first. Turn. Chain, 4d, join to small picot of first chain, 5d, then 9p with 2d between each, 5d, small picot and 4d. Continue, making second clover like first.

No. 42.—Ring, 4d, p, 4d, p, 4d, close. Turn. Tie on second thread. Chain 8d, p, 5d, then 6p with 3d between each, 8d, p, then ring, 4d, 4p with 2d between each, 2d, join to picot of first small ring, 2d, p, 2d, p, 4d, close. Turn. Chain 2d. Turn. ring, 5d, join, 2d, then 4p with 2d between each, 5d, close. Ring, 5d, join, 2d, then 4p with 2d between each, 5d, close. This completes middle ring of clover. Repeat two rings as on other side. Turn. Chain 8d, join to last picot of chain first made and continue as in first chain.

No. 43.—Make ring, 10d, long picot 10d, close. Tie on second thread. Turn. Chain 4d, p, 4d, p, 4d, p, 4d. ring, like first, joining in long picot. Continue making this ring and this chain until five rings, each joined in the long picot, form the cluster. Turn, chain 5d, then 5p with 3d between each, 5d. Repeat.

No. 44.—Starting in clover leaf, ring, 5d, p, 6d, p, 3d, p, 6d, p, 5d, close. Second Ring. 5d join, 3d, p, 6d, p, 6d, p, 3d, p, 5d, close. Third Ring like first. Tie on second thread. Turn. Chain 5d, p, 5d, p, 3d, p, 3d, p, 5d.—Small picot—5d, join to picot of third ring of clover, 5d, small picot, 5d. Turn. Ring, 5d, join to picot of large ring of clover, 5d, p, 5d, close. Turn. Chain, 5d. Repeat first clover leaf, joining to last p of small ring. Turn. Chain 5d. Ring, 5d, join, 5d, p, 5d, close. Turn. Chain 5d, join to small picot in corresponding chain, 5d, turn, make 1p (thus bringing on inside of chain),—turn, 5d, join to picot of chain, 5d, p, 5d, p, 3d, p, 5d, small picot, 5d. Repeat from start, joining second picot of first ring to the turned picot in the chain. Second Row. Make chain of 5d and p, joining to every picot of upper chain.

No. 45.—Ring 7d, p, 1d, p, six times, 2d, close. Tie on second thread, Turn. Chain 5 d, p, 4d, p, 5d, p, 5d, and join to sixth picot of ring, 5d, p, 7d, p, Turn. Make three rings like first without leaving any space. Turn, chain 7d, join to picot of last chain. 5d, p (turned back as shown at end of work), 5d, join to next picot, 5d, p, 4d, p, 5d. Another ring, joining second picot to turned picot of chain. Repeat from start, joining center picots of first and last rings of top cluster.

No. 46.—Start clover leaf. Ring 5d, p, 3d, p, 3d, p, 5d, close. Large ring, 7d, join, 3d, 5p, with 2d between each, 3d, p, 7d, close. Make third ring like first, joining to last picot made. Tie on second thread. Turn. Chain, 5d, p, 3d, p, 3d, p, 5d. Ring 5d, p, 3d, join, 3d, p, 5d, close. Make same ring opposite with the three picots then chain 7 and duplicate these two rings joining to picots as shown. Turn. Chain 7. Turn. large ring, 7d, join to center picot of small ring, 3d, p, 2d, p, 1d, p, 3d, p, 7d. Turn. Chain 7 and follow design.

No. 47.—Ring, 2d, p, 2d, then 8p with 2d between each, 2d, close. Tie on second thread. Turn. Chain 7d, p, 5d, p, 5d, p, 7d, join to fifth picot of ring. Repeat from start. Second Row: join two threads to first picot of chain. Chain 5d, p, 2d, then 4p with 2d between each, 3d, join to third picot of first chain above, 5d, join to first picot of second chain. Turn. ring, 2d, 5p with 2d between each, 2d, close. Turn. chain, 5d, join to last picot of first chain, 2d then 4p with 2d between each, 3d, join to center picot of ring last made, 5d. Turn. ring, 2d, p, 1d, then 4p with 1d between each, 2d, close. Turn. chain 5d, small picot, 3d, p, 2d then 6p with 2d between each, 4d. Turn. ring, 2d, p, 2d, p, 2d, picot into small picot of chain, 2d, p, 2d, p, 2d, close. Turn. chain 1d, join to third picot of chain above, 4d join to first picot of next chain. Repeat from start.

41

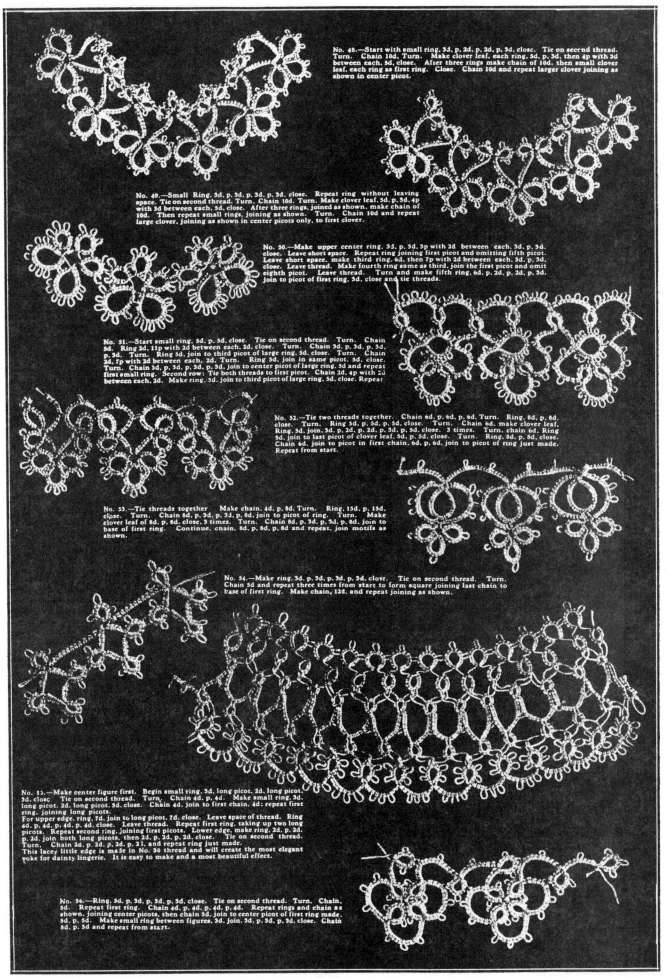

No. 48.—Start with small ring, 3d, p, 2d, p, 2d, p, 3d, close. Tie on second thread. Turn. Chain 10d, Turn. Make clover leaf, each ring, 5d, p, 3d, p, 3d between each, 5d, close. After three rings make chain of 10d, then small clover leaf, each ring as first ring. Close. Chain 10d and repeat larger clover joining as shown in center picot.

No. 49.—Small Ring, 5d, p, 5d, p, 5d, p, 5d, close. Repeat ring without leaving space. Tie on second thread. Turn. Chain 10d. Turn. Make clover leaf, 5d, p, 5d, 4p with 3d between each, 5d, close. After three rings, joined as shown, make chain of 10d. Then repeat small rings, joining as shown. Turn. Chain 10d and repeat large clover, joining as shown in center picots only, to first clover.

No. 50.—Make upper center ring, 3d, p, 3d, 3p with 2d between each, 3d, p, 5d, close. Leave short space. Repeat ring joining first picot and omitting fifth picot. Leave short space, make third ring, 6d, then 7p with 2d between each, 3d, p, 5d, close. Leave thread. Make fourth ring same as third, join the first picot and omit eighth picot. Leave thread. Turn and make fifth ring, 6d, p, 2d, p, 5d, join to picot of first ring, 3d, close and tie threads.

No. 51.—Start small ring, 5d, p, 5d, close. Tie on second thread. Turn. Chain 5d. Ring 2d, 11p with 2d between each, 2d, close. Turn. Chain 3d, p, 3d, p, 3d. Turn. Ring 5d, join to third picot of large ring, 5d, close. Turn. Chain 2d, 7p with 2d between each, 2d, Turn. Ring 5d, join in same picot, 5d, close. Turn. Chain 3d, p, 3d, p, 3d, p, 3d, join to center picot of large ring, 5d and repeat first small ring. Second row: Tie both threads to first picot. Chain 2d, 4p with 2d between each, 2d. Make ring, 5d, join to third picot of large ring, 5d, close. Repeat

No. 52.—Tie two threads together. Chain 6d, p, 6d, p, 6d, Turn. Ring, 8d, p, 8d, close. Turn. Ring 5d, p, 5d, p, 5d, close. Turn. Chain 6d, make clover leaf, Ring, 5d, join, 3d, p, 2d, p, 2d, p, 3d, p, 5d, close. 3 times. Turn, chain 6d, Ring 5d, join to last picot of clover leaf, 5d, p, 5d, close. Turn. Ring, 8d, p, 8d, close. Chain 6d, join to picot in first chain, 6d, p, 6d, join to picot of ring just made. Repeat from start.

No. 53.—Tie threads together. Make chain, 4d, p, 8d, Turn. Ring, 15d, p, 15d, close. Turn. Chain 8d, p, 3d, p, 3d, p, 8d, join to picot of ring. Turn. Make clover leaf of 8d, p, 8d, close, 3 times. Turn. Chain 8d, p, 3d, p, 3d, p, 8d, join to base of first ring. Continue, chain, 8d, p, 8d, p, 8d and repeat, join motifs as shown.

No. 54.—Make ring, 3d, p, 3d, p, 3d, p, 3d, close. Tie on second thread. Turn. Chain 5d and repeat three times from start to form square joining last chain to base of first ring. Make chain, 12d, and repeat joining as shown.

No. 55.—Make center figure first. Begin small ring, 3d, long picot, 2d, long picot, 3d, close. Tie on second thread. Turn. Chain 4d, p, 4d. Make small ring, 3d, long picot, 2d, long picot, 3d, close. Chain 4d, join to first chain, 4d; repeat first ring, joining long picots.
For upper edge, ring, 7d, join to long picot, 7d, close. Leave space of thread. Ring 4d, p, 4d, p, 4d, p, 4d, close. Leave thread. Repeat first ring, taking up two long picots. Repeat second ring, joining first picots. Lower edge, make ring, 2d, p, 2d, p, 2d, join both long picots, then 2d, p, 2d, p, 2d, close. Tie on second thread. Turn. Chain 2d, p, 2d, p, 2d, p, 2l, and repeat ring just made.
This lacey little edge is made in No. 30 thread and will create the most elegant yoke for dainty lingerie. It is easy to make and a most beautiful effect.

No. 56.—Ring, 3d, p, 3d, p, 3d, p, 3d, close. Tie on second thread. Turn. Chain, 5d. Repeat first ring. Chain 4d, p, 4d, p, 4d, p, 4d. Repeat rings and chain as shown, joining center picots, then chain 5d, join to center picot of first ring made, 5d, p, 5d. Make small ring between figures, 3d, join, 3d, p, 3d, p, 3d, close. Chain 8d, p, 5d and repeat from start.

All pieces shown on this page are a number 30 thread unless otherwise noted. Instructions for making rings always means using the shuttle thread and making chains means using the ball thread.

No. 57.—Start lower figure. Make ring, chain 10d. long picot, 10d. close. Tie on second thread. Turn. Chain 4d. p. 4d. p. 4d. p. 4d. p. 4d. Make ring like first, joining into long picot. Complete one whole motif of chains and rings. After fifth ring, start lower ring of upper figure and complete in same manner. In the third motif the first chain joins center picots with the first motif.

No. 58.—Start center clover. Make ring, 4d. p. 5d. p. 5d. p. 2d. p. 2d. p. 5d. p. 5d. p. 4d. close. Repeat. Join first picot to 5th picot of ring just made. Complete five rings. Second Row: Ring 2d. p. 2d. join to fourth picot of large ring, 2d. p. 2d. close. Leave quarter inch thread. Make large outer ring, 5d. p. 5d. p. 2d. p. 2d. p. 5d. p. 5d. close. Leave quarter inch thread. Ring 2d. join, 2d. p. 2d. p. 2d. close. Always leave thread between rings. Continue large rings joining first picots and small rings likewise. Every third small ring joining to center picot of cloverleaf. In joining motifs, join the three picots of the upper outer ring.

No. 59.—Make upper half, around outer corner, and down, as follows: Ring 5d. p. 5d. p. 5d. p. 5d. close. Tie on second thread. Turn. Chain 5d. then 5p with 2d between each, 5d. Turn. Ring, 5d. p. 5d. join to center picot, 5d. p. 5d. close. Chain 5d. Repeat ring and chain and ring. Then start first ring of corner design, 5d. p. 5d. p. 5d. p. 5d. close. Then chain as before, making group of four rings joined by middle picot. Continue same chain and rings. Lower Row: First and second figures as above, joining only center picot of rings. Then to make turn, chain 5d. p. 5d. Make first ring down side, 5d. p. 5d. join to picots of outer rings, 5d. p. 5d. close. Chain 5d. join to first picot of chain, 4p with 2d between, 5d. close. Continue rings and chains down side.

No. 60.—The upper chain on this design is crocheted. Chain 2, 1 double crochet in the third picot of first ring. Chain 6, 1 tr. tr. in fifth picot drawing thread through needle three times and leaving two loops on needle. 1 treble cr. in picot of medallion and draw twice through loops on needle. Chain about 8, 1dc into picot of medallion, chain about 8 and join as between first ring and medallion. Medallion motif: Center ring, 2d. 8p with 2d between, close. Small rings, 5d. join to center picots, 5d. close. Tie on second thread. Turn. Chain 5d. p. 5d. Repeat this ring and chain around the eight picots. Start outer rings, 7d. 5p. with 2d between each, 7d. close. Tie on second thread. Turn. Chain 6d. Turn. Ring 2d. p. 2d. p. 2d. p. 2d. p. 2d. join to picot of medallion. 2d. p. 2d. p. 2d. p. 2d. close. Turn. Chain 5d. then 5p with 2d between each, 5d. Repeat ring and repeat chain. Repeat ring to medallion. Make lower ring opposite this, 5d. 7p with 2d between each, 5d. close. Follow same work around other side.

No. 61.—Ring 5d. p. 3d. p. 3d. p. 3d. close. Leave quarter inch thread. Ring 5d. join to picot of first ring, 4d. p. 4d. p. 3d. Leave quarter inch thread. Make third ring like second. Fourth ring: 4d. join. 4d. p. 4d. p. 4d. Fifth ring: 4d. join. 5d. p. 5d. p. 4d. Sixth ring: 5d. join. 5d. p. 5d. p. 5d. Seventh ring: 5d. join. 6d. p. 6d. p. 5d. Lower center ring, 6d. join. 2d. 6p with 2d between 6d. close. Then work back from seventh to first ring.
Top Row: Tie two threads to picot of top ring, chain 2d. turn. ring 5d. p. then 1d. p. four times, 5d. close. Continue chain 2d. join to picot of next ring. 4d. join to picot of next ring. Repeat from start.

43

No. 62—These 2 squares are the same design, made in No. 70 and in No. 30. Motif: Make and join 4 rings; 6d, then 6p with 2d between each, 6d, close. Make next ring without leaving any space, joining first p to last p of first ring. Repeat joining last picot of 4th ring to first picot of first ring. 2nd Row: Ring, 5d, join to picot of first ring 5d, close. Tie on second thread, turn, chain 5d, p, 5d. Another ring like last and repeat around first motif, joining last chain to 1st ring.

In the YOKE this same motif is used with the addition of this Third Row: Make clover leaf: First Ring, 2d, then 5p with 2d between each 2d, close. Second Ring, 3d, join to last p of first ring 2d, p, 1d, join to corner of first motif, 1d, p, 2d, p, 3d, close. Third Ring, like first. Tie on second thread, turn, chain, 3d, 3p with 3d betw each 3d. Make ring like last joined to next picot of chain. Repeat, making clover leaf at each corner, and 3 small rings between.

No. 63—Ring, 9d, p, 9d, close. Tie on second thread, turn, chain, 3d, p, 3d, p, 3d, p, 3d. Turn, ring 9d, join to first ring, 9d, close. Make 2 more rings to form clover leaf. Turn, chain, 3d, join to chain opposite, 5d, p, 5d, p, 5d. Turn, ring, 9d, join to last ring made, 9d, close. Turn, chain, 3d, 3p with 3d betw each, 3d and make another clover. When desired length make second row in same manner, middle rings joining clovers.

No. 64—Ring, 8d, p, 8d, close. Tie on second thread, turn, chain, 5d, p, 5d, p, 5d. Repeat 3 times, joining picots of rings and forming small square. Make 3 more small squares joining as shown.

No. 65—Ring. 3d, then 5p with 3d betw each, 3d, close. Tie on second thread, turn, chain, 3d, 5p with 3d betw each, 3d. Turn, make second ring like first joining picot as shown. Continue around to form medallion.

No. 66—Ring 2d, 14p with 2d betw each, close, break thread. Ring 4d, join to p of center ring, 4d close. Leave 1/4 in thread and make outer ring, 5d, 5p with 3d between each, 5d close, leave thread and repeat, joining picots as shown.

No. 67—Ring, 4d, p, 3d, p, 2d, p, 3d, p, 4d, close. Make 4 rings joining first picot of each. Second Row: Tie 2 threads on picot of ring, chain 3d to second picot of same ring. Chain 3d, p, 2d, p, 2d, p, 3d to picot of second ring, repeat around. Third Row: Tie 2 threads to first picot of chain, chain 11d, p, 8d, small picot (or loose stitch), 8d, join, 11d, join to third picot on 2nd row, continue chain, 5d, p, 3d, 4p with 3d betw each, 5d, bring chain around back of work and join to same picot as last used. Continue around. Fourth Row: Tie two threads to loose stitch or small picot, 3d, then 3p with 3d betw each, 3d, join to center picot of ring made by chain. Then same chain to next loose stitch.

No. 68—Ring, 6d, p, 3d, p, 3d, p, 6d, close. Second Ring. 7d, p, 4d, p, 7d, close. Third ring like first, and fourth ring like second. Repeat 3 times, joining as shown. Second Row—Ring 6d, p, 6d, join to center picot of motif, 6d, p, 6d, close. Tie on second thread, turn, chain, 5d, 7p, with 3d betw each, 5d. Turn, ring, 6d, p, 6d, join, 6d, p, 6d, close. Turn, chain, 5d, 5p with 3d betw each, 5d. Then middle ring, 8d, join, 8d, join, 8d, close. Turn, chain 5d, 5p with 3d betw each, 5d, repeat.

This medallion matches edging No. 75, on opposite page.

No. 69—Make and join 6 rings, 2d, 3p with 2d betw each, 2d, close, joining third picot of last ring to first p of first ring. Tie and cut. Second Row: 2d, 3p with 2d between each, 2d, close. Tie on second thread, turn, chain, 7d. Turn, ring, 7d, join to small ring just made, 4d join to center motif, 4d, p, 7d, close. Ring, 2d, 5p with 1d betw each, 2d: close. Turn, chain 7d, and repeat.

No. 70—Ring 2d, long picot, 3d, long picot 7 times, 1d, close tie and cut thread. Tie two threads to picot, chain 3d, turn, ring 2d, 3p with 1d betw each, 2d close. Turn, chain 3d to next picot. Repeat. Second Row: Continue chain, 7d, 3p with 7d betw each, 7d. join to next picot. Repeat. Third Row: Ring 1d then 5p with 1d betw each, 1d, close, join to center picot of last chain, tie on second thread turn, chain 3d, repeat last ring, joined by first picot. Repeat chain and ring 5 times in all, join to next point and continue around, joining last chain to base of ring.

No. 71—Make ring, 1d, 12 very long—(1/2-inch)—picots, with 2d betw each, 1d, close, tie. Second Row: Tie two threads to last picot, chain 2d, 3p with 1d betw each, 2d, join to next long picot. Repeat. Third Row: Join last picot of chain to first picot of next chain, and chain 3d, p, 2d. Turn, ring, 1d, 7p with 1d betw each, 1d, close. Turn, chain, 2d, p, 3d, skipping a picot, join to next 2 picots. Repeat.

This medallion matches edging No. 76.

No. 72—Make 4 rings—(for 4 motifs)—of 2d, 10 long picots, with 2d betw each, 2d, close, tie, cut thread. Second Row: Tie 2 threads to first picot made, chain 4d, p, 4d, join to next long picot, repeat around. Third Row: Continue this chain, 4d, p, 3d, p, 4d, join to first long picot of another ring; chain 4d, join to picot in last chain of first motif. 4d, join to next long picot of new motif and continue same way around. Outer Row: Ring 6d, join to last open picot of first motif, 2d, join to corresponding picot of next motif, 6d, close. Tie on second thread, turn, chain, 4d, p, 4d, join to next picot and continue around.

This medallion matches edging No. 77.

No. 73—Ring, 8d, p, 8d, close. Tie on second thread, turn, chain, 1d, then 9p with 2d between each, join to picot of ring, 1d, 9p with 2d betw each, join to base of ring. Tie and cut threads. Second Row: Ring, 6d, join to 2nd picot of chain, 6d, close. Tie on second thread, turn, chain, 3d, 3p with 2d betw each, 3d. Make ring like last, continue chain and ring, joining at every other picot, and join last chain to first ring, tie and cut. Third Row: Ring, 4d, join to middle picot of last ring, 4d, p, 8d, close. Tie on second thread, turn, chain, 2d, then 8p with 2d betw each, 2d, join to base of ring last made. Leave space length of picot, repeat ring and chain around, last chain joins first ring.

45

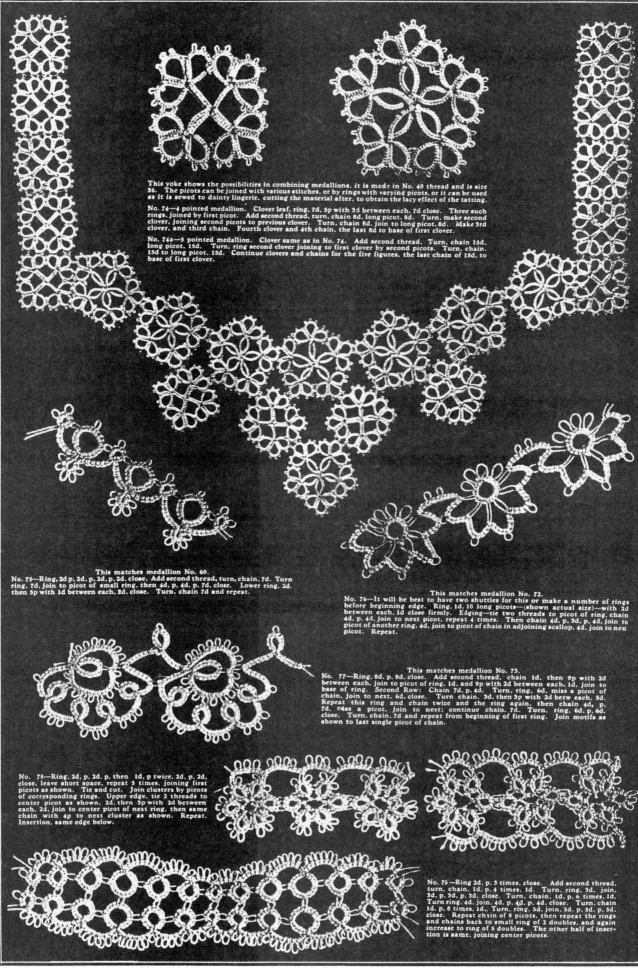

This yoke shows the possibilities in combining medallions, it is made in No. 40 thread and is size 36. The picots can be joined with various stitches, or by rings with varying picots, or it can be used as it is sewed to dainty lingerie, cutting the material after, to obtain the lacy effect of the tatting.

No. 74—4 pointed medallion. Clover leaf, ring, 7d, 5p with 3d between each, 7d close. Three such rings, joined by first picot. Add second thread, turn, chain 8d, long picot, 8d. Turn, make second clover, joining second picots to previous clover. Turn, chain 8d, join to long picot, 8d. Make 3rd clover, and third chain. Fourth clover and 4th chain, the last 8d to base of first clover.

No. 74a—5 pointed medallion. Clover same as in No. 74. Add second thread, Turn, chain 15d, long picot, 15d. Turn, ring second clover joining to first clover by second picots. Turn, chain, 15d to long picot, 15d. Continue clovers and chains for the five figures, the last chain of 15d, to base of first clover.

This matches medallion No. 69.
No. 75—Ring, 2d p, 2d, p, 2d, p, 2d, p, 2d, close. Add second thread, turn, chain, 7d. Turn ring, 7d, join to picot of small ring, then 4d, p, 4d, p, 7d, close. Lower ring. 2d, then 5p with 1d between each, 2d, close. Turn, chain 7d and repeat.

This matches medallion No. 72.
No. 76—It will be best to have two shuttles for this or make a number of rings before beginning edge. Ring, 1d, 10 long picots—(shown actual size)—with 2d between each, 1d close firmly. Edging—tie two threads to picot of ring, chain 4d, p, 4d, join to next picot, repeat 4 times. Then chain 4d, p, 3d, p, 4d, join to picot of another ring, 4d, join to picot of chain in adjoining scallop, 4d, join to next picot. Repeat.

This matches medallion No. 73.
No. 77—Ring, 8d, p, 8d, close. Add second thread, chain 1d, then 9p with 2d between each, join to picot of ring, 1d, and 9p with 2d between each, 1d, join to base of ring. Second Row: Chain 7d, p, 4d. Turn, ring, 6d, miss a picot of chain, join to next, 6d, close. Turn, chain, 3d, then 3p with 2d betw each, 3d. Repeat this ring and chain twice and the ring again, then chain 4d, p, 7d, miss a picot, join to next; continue chain, 7d. Turn, ring, 6d, p, 6d, close. Turn, chain, 7d and repeat from beginning of first ring. Join motifs as shown to last single picot of chain.

No. 78—Ring, 2d, p, 2d, p, then 1d, p twice, 2d, p, 2d, close, leave short space, repeat 5 times, joining first picots as shown. Tie and cut. Join clusters by picots of corresponding rings. Upper edge, tie 2 threads to center picot as shown, 2d, then 3p with 2d between each, 2d, join to center picot of next ring, then same chain with 4p to next cluster as shown. Repeat. Insertion, same edge below.

No. 79—Ring 2d, p, 3 times, close. Add second thread, turn, chain, 1d, p, 4 times, 1d. Turn, ring, 3d, p, 3d, p, 3d, close. Turn, chain, 1d, p, 6 times, 1d. Turn ring, 4d, join, 4d, p, 4d, p, 4d, close. Turn, chain 1d, p, 6 times, 1d, join, 5d, p, 5d, p, 5d, close. Repeat chain of 6 picots, then repeat the rings and chains back to small ring of 2 doubles, and again increase to ring of 5 doubles. The other half of insertion is same, joining center picots.

46

No. 81.—The Handkerchiefs shown on this page are very simple and dainty. They are easily made and the motifs are as follows:
Using No. 70 thread, the dark edge is 4d. p. repeated joining the side picots.

No. 82. The double row kerchief is in No. 30 white and No. 50 light blue. The ring is white and one chain blue. Ring 4d. p. 4d. p. 8d. close. Tie on blue thread. Chain 8d. p. 8d. join to second picot of ring.
These kerchiefs make a most beautiful finished gift and are always considered a proud possession.

No. 80 This dainty yoke is made of the simple Dixie insertion, variations of which are shown on earlier pages. It is so easy that it is a delight to the worker and makes up most beautifully in a yoke for corset cover, envelope chemise or night gown.
The motif is 4d. p. 4d. p. 4d. p. 4d. close. Tie on second thread. Chain 4d. Ring 4d. p. 4d. p. 4d. p. 4d. close. Turn. chain 4d. Ring 4d. join to first ring, then 4d. p. 4d. p. 4d.
For the clover leaf edge the motif is 4d. p. 3d. p. 3d. p. 4d. close. Second ring: 4d. join. 4d. p. 4d. p. 4d. close. Third ring, 4d. join third picot. 3d. p. 3d. p. 4d. close. The same motif is applied to the sleeve bands which are shown. The total number of single rings in one row from one shoulder point to another is ninety-three and in No. 40 thread, this makes about size 36. It can, of course, be adapted to any variation desired for other sizes, and more or less points added if desired.

47

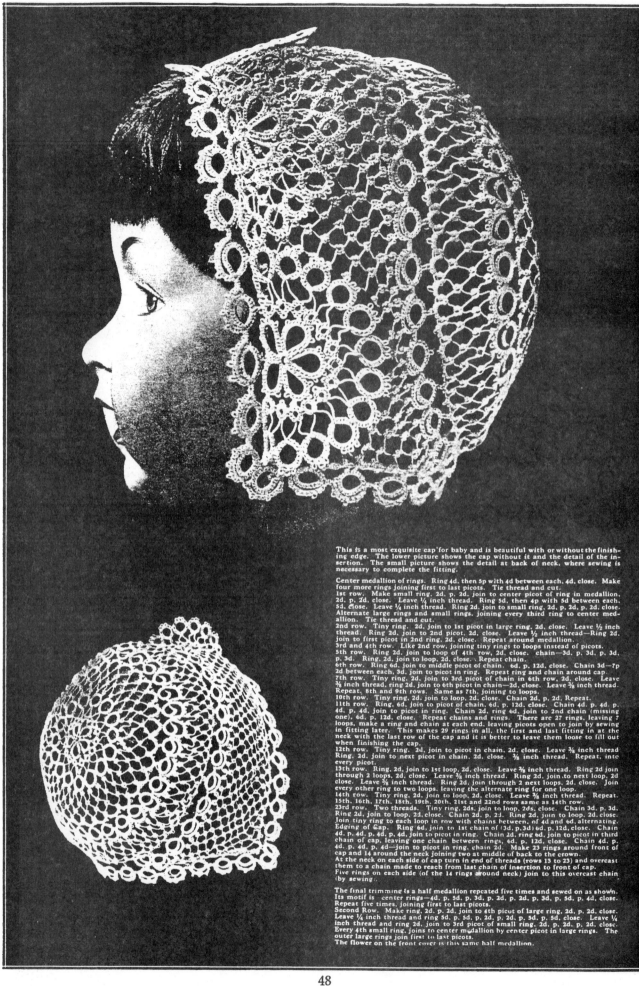

This is a most exquisite cap for baby and is beautiful with or without the finishing edge. The lower picture shows the cap without it and the detail of the insertion. The small picture shows the detail at back of neck, where sewing is necessary to complete the fitting.

Center medallion of rings. Ring 4d, then 5p with 4d between each, 4d, close. Make four more rings joining first to last picots. Tie thread and cut.

1st row. Make small ring, 2d, p, 2d, join to center picot of ring in medallion, 2d, p, 2d, close. Leave ¼ inch thread. Ring 5d, then 4p with 5d between each, 5d, close. Leave ¼ inch thread. Ring 2d, join to small ring, 2d, p, 2d, p, 2d, close. Alternate large rings and small rings, joining every third ring to center medallion. Tie thread and cut.

2nd row. Tiny ring. 2d, join to 1st picot in large ring, 2d, close. Leave ½ inch thread. Ring 2d, join to 2nd picot, 2d, close. Leave ½ inch thread—Ring 2d, join to first picot in 2nd ring, 2d, close. Repeat around medallion.

3rd and 4th row. Like 2nd row, joining tiny rings to loops instead of picots.

5th row. Ring 2d, join to loop of 4th row, 2d, close. chain—3d, p, 3d, p, 3d, p, 3d. Ring, 2d, join to loop, 2d, close. Repeat chain.

6th row. Ring 6d, join to middle picot of chain. 6d, p, 12d, close. Chain 3d—7p 2d between each, 3d, join to picot in ring. Repeat ring and chain around cap.

7th row. Tiny ring, 2d, join to 3rd picot of chain in 6th row, 2d, close. Leave ⅜ inch thread, ring 2d, join to 6th picot in chain—2d, close. Leave ⅜ inch thread. Repeat, 8th and 9th rows. Same as 7th, joining to loops.

10th row. Tiny ring. 2d, join to loop, 2d, close. Chain 2d, p, 2d, Repeat.

11th row. Ring, 6d, join to picot of chain, 6d, p, 12d, close. Chain 4d. p. 4d. p. 4d. p. 4d, join to picot in ring. Chain 2d, ring 6d, join to 2nd chain (missing one), 6d, p, 12d, close. Repeat chains and rings. There are 27 rings, leaving 7 loops, make a ring and chain at each end, leaving picots open to join by sewing in fitting later. This makes 29 rings in all, the first and last fitting in at the neck with the last row of the cap and it is better to leave them loose to fill out when finishing the cap.

12th row. Tiny ring. 2d, join to picot in chain, 2d, close. Leave ⅜ inch thread Ring. 2d, join to next picot in chain, 2d, close. ⅜ inch thread. Repeat, into every picot.

13th row. Ring, 2d, join to 1st loop, 2d, close. Leave ⅜ inch thread. Ring 2d join through 2 loops, 2d, close. Leave ⅜ inch thread. Ring 2d, join.to next loop, 2d close. Leave ⅜ inch thread. Ring 2d, join through 2 next loops, 2d, close. Join every other ring to two loops, leaving the alternate ring for one loop.

14th row. Tiny ring, 2d, join to loop, 2d, close. Leave ⅜ inch thread. Repeat.

15th, 16th, 17th, 18th, 19th, 20th, 21st and 22nd rows same as 14th row.

23rd row. Two threads. Tiny ring, 2ds, join to loop, 2ds, close. Chain 3d, p, 3d. Ring 2d, join to loop, 2d, close. Chain 2d, p, 2d. Ring 2d, join to loop, 2d, close. Join tiny ring to each loop in row with chains between, of 4d and 6d, alternating.

Edging of Cap. Ring 6d, join to 1st chain of (3d, p,3d) 6d p, 12d, close. Chain 4d. p. 4d. p. 4d. p. 4d, join to picot in ring. Chain 2d, ring 6d, join to picot in third chain of cap, leaving one chain between rings, 6d, p, 12d, close. Chain 4d. p. 4d. .p. 4d. p. 4d—join to picot in ring, chain 2d. Make 23 rings around front of cap and 14 around the neck joining two at middle of back to the crown.

At the neck on each side of cap turn in end of threads (rows 13 to 23) and overcast them to a chain made to reach from last chain of insertion to front of cap. Five rings on each side (of the 14 rings around neck) join to this overcast chain (by sewing).

The final trimming is a half medallion repeated five times and sewed on as shown. Its motif is center rings—4d, p, 5d, p, 3d, p, 2d, p, 2d, p, 3d, p, 5d, p, 4d, close. Repeat five times, joining first to last picots.

Second Row. Make ring, 2d, p, 2d, join to 4th picot of large ring, 2d, p, 2d, close. Leave ¼ inch thread and ring 5d, p, 5d, p, 2d, p, 2d, p, 5d, p, 5d, close. Leave ¼ inch thread and ring 2d, join to 3rd picot of small ring, 2d. p, 2d, p, 2d, close. Every 4th small ring, joins to center medallion by center picot in large rings. The outer large rings join first to last picots.

The flower on the front cover is this same half medallion.

A Ch. 10d. turn. Ring 12d turn. Ch 4d, p. 9d. Ring 6d. Ch 8d, p, 7d, join to center of first ring. 10d, reverse chain, then 17d, p, 9d, tie where chain was reversed.

B Ring 10d, p, 6d. Chain 13d, small picot, 8d. Ring 6d, p. Ch 12d, p, 8d, turn. Ring 6d, join to small picot, 6d. Ch 10d, p, 16d, join to 4th stitch from first ring, chain 9d, tie threads together and cut.

C Ring 10d, p, 8d. Ch 19d. Ring 8d, p, 8d. Ch 26d, p, 11d, join to first ch as shown, 10d, turn. Ring 11d, p, 10d.

D Ch 5d, small picot, 6d, p, 6d. Ring 6d, p, 6d. Ch 13d, p, 24d. Ring 22d, join to small picot, 9d, close.

E Ring 7d, p, 8d. Ch 9d, p, 6d. Ring 6d. Ch 9d, p, 22d. Ring 9d, p, 8d, p, 9d, close-tie and cut threads.

F Ring 7d, p, 6d. Chain 11d. Ring 4d, p, 4d. Ch 11d. Make 2 rings opposite each other of 8d. Ch 19d. Ring 6d, p, 5d, p, 6d close, tie and cut threads.

G Ring 10d, p, 5d,, p, 8d close. Ch 20d. Ring 9d, p, 5d. Ch 16d, p, 13d, join to p of last ring made, 6d join at sixth stitch from ring, 5d, tie and cut.

H Ring 9d, p, 9d. Ring 4d, small p, 4d. Ch 8d. Ring 6d, p, 9d –tie and cut threads. Make other half same joining small rings at picots.

I Ring 9d, p, 9d. Ch 25d, p, 8d, p, 7d, join to center of long chain, 3d, tie and cut threads.

J Ch 8d. turn. Ring 7d. turn. Ch 30d, p, 8d, p, 7d, join a little above center of long chain, 3d—tie and cut threads. Join ends at same place.

K Ring 6d, p, 9d. Ch 9d. Ring 3d, small picot, 3d. Ch 8d. Ring 9d, p, 6d, close, tie and cut threads. Second half. Ring 6d, p, 9d. Ch 19d. join to small ring, 17d. Ring 9d, p, 6d close, tie and cut threads.

L Ring 7d, p, 6d. Ch 12d. Ring 5d, turn. Ch 9d, turn. Ring 11d, p, 7d. Ch 9d, turn. Ring 7d, p, 11d. Tie and cut.

M Ring 9d, p, 6d. Ch 10d, p, 10d. Ring 5d. Ch 19d. Ring 5d. Ch 20d. Ring 5d. Ch 18d. Ring 6d, p, 9d, close and cut. Keep all chain turned toward front.

N Ring 9d, p, 6d. Ch 11d, p, 11d. Ring 5d. Ch 21d. Ring 5d. Ch 8d, p, 3d. Ring 9d, p, 6d, p, close, tie and cut threads.

O Ring 14d, p, 22d close. Ch 23d. turn. Ring 5d. turn. Ch 13d. Ring 5d. Ch 12d. Count back on large ring 7d from start of chain. Tie and cut threads.

P Ring 10, p, 9d. Ch 13d, small picot, 8d, small p, 3d. Ring 6d, p, 6d, turn. Ch 18d, p, 10d, join to first ch at first small picot, 7d. Ring 4d, join to next small picot, 4d.

Q Ring 9d, p, 6d. Ch 5d. Ring 9d, p, 9d, turn. Ch 5d, join to p of first ring, 19d. Ring 11d, p, 9d, p, 11d. Tie and cut.

R Ring 6d, p, 6d, turn. Ch 12d. Ring 17d, turn .Ch 7d, p, 12d. Ring 6d, p, 6d. Ch 7d, join to center large ring as shown, 2d, join to other side, 13d, turn.

S Ring 5d, p, 13d, turn. Ch 17d, p, 6d, turn. Ch 12d, p, 11d, tie where chain is turned, 9d, p, 9d. ie and cut threads.

T Ring 7d, p, 6d. Ch 11d. Ring 4d, p, 4d. Ch 33d, turn Ring 6d, p, 5d, p, 6d, close– tie and cut threads.

U Ring 4d, p, 4d, p, 4d, p, 4d close. Ch 5d, turn, join to side picot of ring, ch 15d, p, 6d, turn. Ring 12d, turn. Ch 16d, tie threads and carry back to 9th stitch, tie, ch 8d Ring 5d, p, 5d close, tie and cut threads.

V Ring 4d, p, 3 times 4d, close. Ch 5d, turn, join to side picot of ring, 15d, p, 6d, turn. Ring 12d, turn. Ch 14d, turn. Ring 8d, turn. Ch 4d, tie and cut threads.

W Ring 9d, p, 10d, p, 5d. Ch 6d, turn, join to picot of ring, ch 7d. Ring 5d, p, 9d. Ch 7d, turn. Ring 5d, p, 5d turn. Ch 5d. Ring 8d, p, 4d. Ch 14d. Ring 6d, p, 9d, close, cut.

X Ring 4d, p, 9d, p, 5d. Ch 6d, join to first picot of ring, 6d, turn, ch 9d, turn. Ring 5d, p, 9d, close, tie and cut. Second half-ring 5d, p, 10d, close. Ch 5d, join to first half where chain is turned, 8d, turn. Ring 10d, p, 5d, close.

Y Ring 5d, p, 10d, p, 5d. Ch 6d, turn, join to picot of ring, 9d, turn. Ring 5d, p, 5d, turn. Ch 19d, tie threads and carry back to 10th stitch, tie, ch 4d. Ring 9d, close. Ch 6d. Ring 21d, close tie and cut threads.

Z Ring 5d, p, 10d, p, 5d close. Ch 7d. Ring 9d, turn. Ch 7d. Ring 6d, p, 6d. Ch 6d. Ring 9d. Ch 10d. Ring 12d, tie.

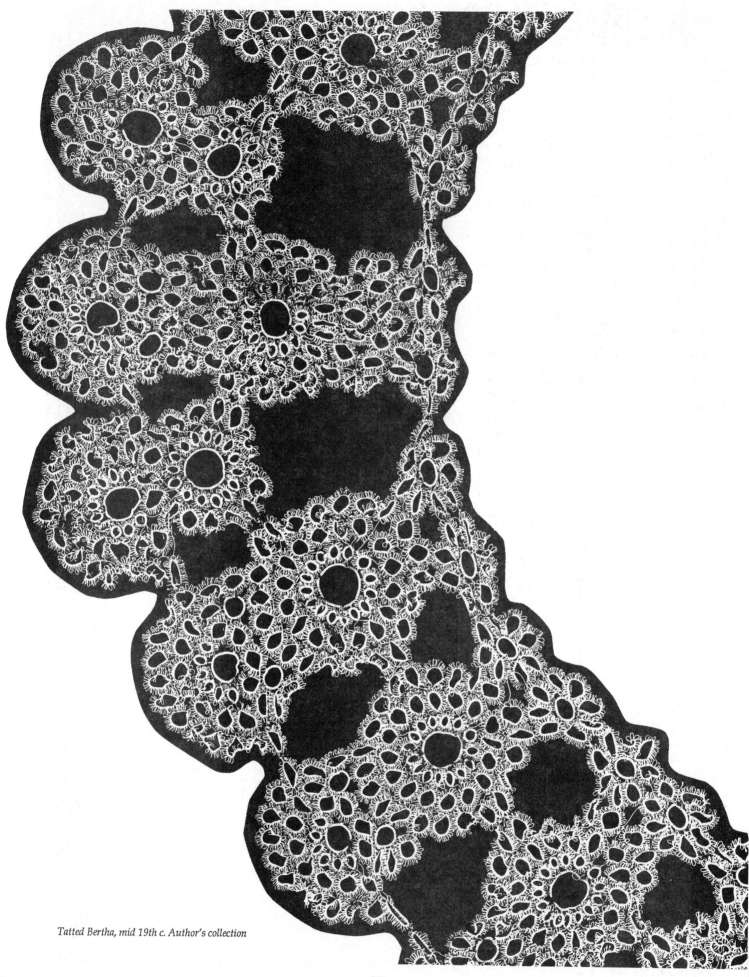

Tatted Bertha, mid 19th c. Author's collection

BOOK
NO FIVE
By
Adeline Cordet

TATTING

DESIGNS
WITH
INSTRUCTIONS

Price
TEN CENTS

"Bon-Bon Basket" & "Butterfly": Instructions on page 51

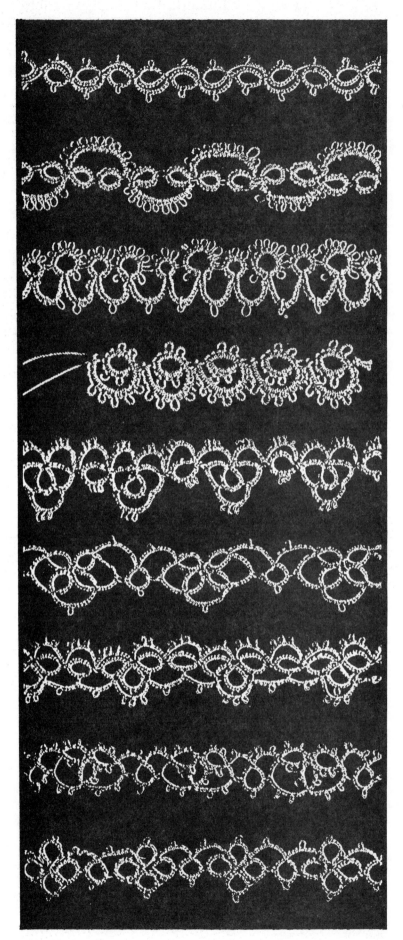

No 500.

R. 10 d. s., p., 5 d. s., p., 5 d. s., close. **2nd Shuttle**—Ch. 7 d. s., p., 7 d. s., fasten to end p. of r. Rep., always having ch. on side of r. without p. and tn. so ch. is on first one side then another.

No. 501.

8 d. s., p., 8 d. s., close; ch. 11 d. s. with 10 p. bet. each d. s., r. 8 d. s., j. to p. in last r., 8 d. s., close; tn. work and ch. on opp. side of work same number of sts. as before. Rep.

No. 502.

4 d. s., p., 10 times, 4 d. s., close; ch. 8 d. s., p., 8 d. s., r. 4 d. s., p., 2 d. s., j. to last p., 2 d. s., p. 4 times, 4 d. s., close. Rep.

No. 504

2 d. s., p., *1 d. s., p., * 4 times, close. 2nd Shuttle—3 d. s., p., * 1 d. s., p. * 4 times, j. to 3rd p. of r.

No 521

*R. 5 d. s., p. * 2 times, 5 d. s., close. **2nd Shuttle**—Ch. 6 d. s., p., 6 d. s., fasten to 1st p. of r., ch. 6 d. s., *p., 1 d. s., * 2 times, p., 6 d. s., fasten to 2nd p., 3rd ch., like 1st, fasten at beginning, ch. 6 d. s., *p., 1 d. s., * 2 times, p., 6 d. s., fasten to p. made on last ch. around r.; rep. this ch., r. 10 d. s., fasten to same p. as 1st outside ch. on top is fastened to, 5 d. s., *p., 1 d. s., * 2 times, p., 5 d. s., make outside top ch. and rep. from first.

No. 547

R. 10 d. s., p., 10 d. s., close; ch. 10 d. s., p., 10 d. s., r. as before joined by p. Rep. until there are 4 rings and 3 chains, ch. 12 d. s., p., 12 d. s. r. 5 d. s., j. to p. on last ch. bet. rings, *5 d. s., p. * 2 times, 5 d. s., rep. ch. of 12 d. s., p., 12 d. s.

No. 548.

Make clover leaf of 3 rings, 10 d. s., p., 5 d. s., p., 5 d. s., close; r. 5 d. s., j. to last p. of preceding r., *5 d. s., p. * 2 times, 5 d. s., close; r. like 1st, j. by 1st p. to last one of middle r., ch. 5 d. s., *p., 2 d. s., * 2 times, p., 5 d. s., fasten to last p. of last r., rep. ch., then r. of 10 d. s., j. to same place as last, 5 d. s., p., 5 d. s., rep. ch. and clover leaf. Form edge by ch. 5 d. s., *p., 2 d. s., * 2 times, p., 5 d. s., fasten to p. on either side of end of middle ring, ch. 5 d. s., p., 5 d. s., fasten to p. on r. bet. clover leaf. Rep. ch. entire length.

No. 561

R. *3 d. s., p. * 5 times, 3 d. s., close; ch. * 5 d. s., p., * 3 times, 5 d. s., rep. r., j. by middle p. of each ch., rep. r., j. as before, ch. * 3 d. s., p., * 2 times, 3 d. s., r. 5 d. s., j. to last p. on last ch. bet. group of 3 rings, *5 d. s., p., * 2 times, 5 d. s., close. Rep. ch. made just before last r., proceed as at first, j. 1st p. on ch. bet. rings to last p. on r. bet. the figures formed by the 3 rings and ch.

No. 562

R. *5 d. s., p., * 3 times, 5 d. s., close; rep. until there is a figure of 4 r., j. by inside p., ch. 5 d. s., p., 5 d. s., r., 5 d. s., j. to p. of last r. made, *5 d. s., p., * 2 times, 5 d. s., close; ch. 5 d. s., p., 5 d. s.; make figure as at 1st, only in making 1st leave thread 1-8-inch long bet. ch. and beginning of r. This can be caught when p.'s of rings are j.

No 570—Rose Yoke.

Make wheels and roses first. 12 of each, joining them alternately each to preceding and last wheel to first rose. **1st Row—** R. *1 d. s., p., 2 d. s., p., * 5 times, 1 d. s., close and tie. Draw spool thread up through 1st p. of r. **2nd Row—**Ch. 7 d. s., j. to next p.; rep., making 6 chs. **3rd Row—**Ch. 9 d. s., draw up until it curves to match the ch. of last row, touching it, j. bet. chs. of last row; rep. **4th Row—**Same as 3rd row with chs. of 10 d. s. **5th Row—**Same as 3rd row with chs. of 11 d. s. **6th Row—**Ch. of 3 d. s., p., 6 d. s., p., 3 d. s., j. bet. chs. of last row; rep. around, tie and cut threads. **7th Row—**Tie threads to 1st p. of ch. of last row, *2 d. s., p., * 5 times, 2 d. s., j. to next, rep. around, tie and cut threads. **Wheel. 1st Row—**R. 5 d. s., p., 5 d. s., close with both threads; make a ch. of *2 d. s., p., 2 d. s., * 5 times; rep. until you have 5 rings and chs., alternating, j. 5th ch. at base of 1st r., tie and fasten. **2nd Row—**R. 5 d. s., j. to 2nd p. of ch. in last row, 5 d. s., close; a ch. as in last row, another r., j. to 4th p. of same ch., a ch., rep., j. 2 r.'s over each ch. of last row. Having made 9 r.'s and 8 chs., j. next ch. by middle p. of ch. in last row of a rose, make a r., j. by 1st free ch. of rose bet. the joining. Make 4 d. s., sk. 1 p. of ch. to which last ch. of rose was j.; j. to next, 4 d. s., p., 4 d. s., close; ch. 5 d. s., a r. like last, j. to latter by 1st side p.; tn., make a r., close to last at the base, j. by 1st p. to middle p. of next ch. of rose, ch. 5 d. s., a r. like preceding, j. to latter by 1st side p., a r. of 4 d. s., j. to last r., *5 d. s., p. * twice, 4 d. s., close a smaller r. like these preceding, j. by side p. of last r. made, a ch. of 5 d. s., a r., j. to preceding by side p.; tn., a r., j. by 1st p. to last p. of opp. r (2nd r. made), ch., 5 d. s., a r., j. by 1st p. to last p. of preceding r. and by 2nd p. to 2nd p. of next ch. of 3rd row (bet. clover leaves); make another r., close to last, j. by 1st to 4th p. of same ch.; rep. from, only j. 3rd r. of pt. to corresponding r. on side of preceding pt. instead of to ch. of rose as at 1st; make 11 pts. j. last to next rose like start. Work pts. bet. each 2 roses in the same way.

Upper Edge on Neck—R. 4 d. s., p., 4 d. s., j. to 2nd p. of 1st free wheel or rose, 4 d. s., p., 4 d. s., close; leave 1-4 in. thread. r. 3 d. s., *p. 3 d. s., * 3 times, close, tn., leave sp. of thread (always), r. 4 d. s., j. to preceding r., 4 d. s., j. to 4th next ch. as directed to next ch. of rose and fasten at base of 1st r., j. all wheels and roses in this way each to preceding and last to 1st. In j. have 3 free chs. of each on upper edge, which leaves 5 free chs. on rose at lower edge and 3 on wheel.

Lower Edge—R. *4 d. s., p. *3 times, 4 d. s., close; 2nd r. of 4 d. s., j. to last p. of 1st r., 5 d. s., j. to middle p. of 1st free ch. of wheel or rose, 5 d. s., p., 4 d. s., close; a 3rd r. like 1st, j. by 1st p. to last p. of preceding r. This completes a clover leaf; ch. 4 d. s., p. *3 d. s., p., * 4 times, 4 d. s.; another clover leaf, j. middle p. of 1st r. to middle p. of 3rd r. of preceding clover leaf and by middle p. of 2nd r. to middle p. of next ch. of wheel, j. a 3rd clover leaf in the same way next to 1st free ch. of rose (always by middle p. of 2nd r. to middle p. of ch.), sk. next ch. of rose, j. a clover leaf to next, sk. next and again j. a clover leaf to next, sk. next and again j. a clover leaf and rep. around, j. 3 clover leaves to each rose and wheel, j. last to 1st and fasten. **2nd Row—**Make 4 roses as previously given, only in 7th row the chs. have 3 p.'s; j. middle p. of a ch. to middle p. of ch. bet. 1st and 2nd clover leaves (j. to wheel) and middle p. of next ch. to middle p. of ch. bet. 2nd and 3rd clover leaves on same wheel; another of 4 roses, j. rose to every 7th wheel. **3rd Row—**J. threads to middle p. of ch., 4 d. s., p., 4 d. s., close, tn., leave sp. of thread, a small r. of 3 d. s., j. to preceding small r., *3 d. s., p. * twice, 3 d. s., close; rep., alternating large and small r.'s; j. each to preceding, j. to large r.'s as directed to next ch. of wheel and 1 to 2nd p. of next bet. wheel and rose; make a free r. large and continue, j. 5 r.'s over each wheel and rose, with free r.'s bet. **4th Row—**R. 3 d. s., j. to p. of small r. of last row, 3 d. s., close; leave sp. of thread, r. 3 d. s., p., *2 d. s., p., * 4 times, 3 d. s., close, tn.; leave sp. of thread, r. 3d. s., j. to middle p. of next small r. of last row, 3 d. s., close, tn.; leave sp., make a large r., j. by 1st p. to last p. of preceding r.; rep., j. last r. to 1st.

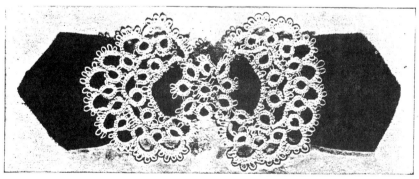

No. 555—Jabot—

Make a r. of 18 d. s. with 8 p. bet., close, cut and tie; r. 4 d. s., p., 3 d. s., 3 p.s., 3 d. s., p.,4 d. s., close; make other joining to last p. each time until there are 8 rings, j. last place for p. to p. in 1st r.; this is center of jabot (for bow end); r. 6 d. s., j. to center p. of center part at edge of r., 6 d. s., close; ch. 12 d. s., r., 6 d. s., skip 1 r. and in center of p.'s join, 6 d. s., close (this is the ch. to slip ribbon through). When all is finished turn work and ch. back 18 d. s., with 8 p. fasten to r., ch., 8 d. s. with 3 p., r. 4 d. s. p., until there are 3 p., 4 d. s., close; ch. 8 as before, r. as before, fastening center of each r. to every other p. above until there are 4 r.; turn work, ch. 10 d. s., with 4 p. r. 3 d. s., p., 3 d. s., j. to p. of last ch., then r., etc., until there are 10 rings and 11 chs.; tie and cut thread. Make another bow same as this and fasten to r. on opp. side of center group of rings, same as one bet. ribbon, and extend an inch from jabot.

No. 508.

R. 3 d.s., p., 2 d.s., p., 2 d.s., p., 3 d.s., close. Ch. 4 d.s., p., ch. 4 d.s., draw up, 3 d.s., j. to last p., 3 d.s., 3 times, p. bet. each, 4 d.s., close. Ch. 4 d.s., p., ch. 4 d.s., r. 4 d.s., j. to last p., 4 d.s., 3 times, close, ch. 2 d.s., tn., r. 4 d.s., 4 times with p. bet. each 4 d.s., close. Ch. 4 d.s., j. p. in opp., ch. 4 d.s., draw up, 3 d.s. j. to last p., 3 d.s., p., 3 d.s., p., 4 d.s., close. Ch. as before j. 4 d.s at p., r. 3 d.s., j. 2 d.s., p., 2 d.s., p., 3 d.s., close. ch. 4 d.s., p., 4 d.s., draw up, R. 3 d.s., j., 2 d.s., p., 2 d.s., p., 3 d.s., close. Continue to length desired then ch. 2 d.s. 6 times with p. bet. each, 2 d.s., j. to 1st p. in ch., 4 d.s. with p. bet. each, 2 d.s., j. to last p. in ch. Rep.

No. 509—2 Shuttles.

*ch. 6 d. s., p. * 3 times, 6 d. s., make clover leaf of 3 rings of *5 d. s., p. * 3 times, 5 d. s., each fastened by inside p., ch. 6 d. s., p., 6 d. s., another clover leaf, rep. ch., clover leaf, ch. 6 d. s., p., 6 d. s., fasten to p. opp., 6 d. s., p., 6 d. s. fasten to 2nd p. of last r., 10 d. s., *p., 1 d. s., * 2 times, p. 10 d. s., make p. on opp. of ch. by turning work. Turn back and rep. from first. Fasten 2nd p. of 1st r. of clover leaf to inside p. on ch.

No. 518.

R. 5 d. s., p., 5 d. s., p. 10 d. s., close. 2nd Shuttle—ch. 10 d. s., *p., 2 d. s., * 2 times, p., 10 d. s., 2nd r. of 10 d. s., j. to last p. of 1st r., 10 d. s., close. Rep. ch. and r. until there are 5 ch. and 6 r., j. last r. to 1st p. made of 1st r., ch. 10 d. s., *p., 2 d. s., * 3 times, p., 10 d. s., r. 10 d. s., j. to p. of last ch. of wheel, *3 d. s., p. * 2 times, 3 d. s., p., 10 d. s., close. Rep. 1 ch., then wheel, j. 2nd p. of 1st short ch. to last p. of r. just made—that is, the r. bet. wheels.

No 545

R. * 5 d. s., p. * 3 times, 5 d. s., close, r. 5 d. s., j. to last p. of preceding r., 5 d. s., p., *2 d. s., p. * 2 times, 5 d. s., p., 5 d. s., close. Rep. 1st r., ch. 6 d. s., r. * 3 d. s., p. * 2 times, 3 d. s., close, ch. d. s., p., 10 d. s., *p., 2 d. s., * 2 times, p., 10 d. s., r. 3 d. s., j. to 1st p. of small r., 3 d. s., p., 3 d. s., close, ch. 10 d. s., *p., 2 d. s., * 2 times, p., 10 d. s., p., 10 d. s., small ring j. by 1st p. to last p. of last r., ch. 6 d. s. Rep.

No. 549.

Ch. 10 d. s., *p., 2 d. s., * 2 times, p., 10 d. s., r. 5 d. s., *p., 2 d. s., * 4 times, p., 5 d. s., close, ch. 10 d. s., p., 10 d. s., r. as before, j. by 1st p. to last p. of preceding r., ch. 10 d. s., 2 ring, j. as before, 10 d. s., r., j., 10 d. s., j. to p. on opp. ch., 10 d. s., r., j., ch. as at 1st, r. as before, j. by 1st p. to last p. of last r.

No. 563.

R. *3 d. s., p. * 7 times, 3 d. s., close, ch. *5 d. s., p. * 4 times, 5 d. s., r. *3 d. s., p. * 9 times, 3 d. s., close, ch. 5 d. s., p., 5 d. s., r. 5 d. s., j. to 1st p. of large r., 5 d. s., close, ch. *3 d. s., p. * 3 times, 3 d. s., small r. as before, j. to 2nd p. of large r., rep. until there are 4 small r. and 4 ch. bet., ch. 5 d. s., p., 5 d. s., j. to 5th p. on large r., *ch. 5 d. s., p. * 4 times, 5 d. s., rep. from 1st.

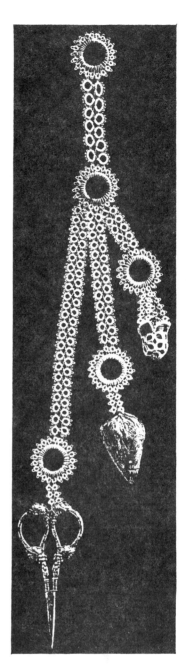

No. 537—Rose Coin Purse.

Begin with center of rose by making r. with 6 p and 2 d. s. bet. each; close. **2nd Shuttle** —Make ch. of 12 d. s. bet. each p., fastening each ch. to a p. In making this ch. make 2nd st. of 1st d. s. loose, so next row of ch. can be fastened to it just above 1st row, which is fastened to p.; 2nd row, ch. 16 d. s., 3rd row, ch. of 20 d. s.; 4th row, 24 d. s.; 5th ow, * 2 d. s., p. * 7 times, 2 d.| s.; 6th row, with 1st shuttle thread, make r. of 2 d. s., j. to 1st p. of 1st ch. of 5th row, 2 d. s., close. Leave thread 1-8 in. and make r. for every other p., making one for 1st and last p. of each ch. Rep. this for 4 rows, j. middle of r. to thread left bet. r. of preceding row. **2nd Shuttle**—Make outside edge of r. of 5 d. s., j. to middle of thread bet. r.'s of preceding row, ch. of 5 d. s., * p. 1 d. s., * 2 times, p., 5 d. s. bet. each r., leaving 7 spaces at top for opening. Both sides can be made alike and fastened together where last row of rings and ch. is fastened on; top is made of r. of 5 d. s., j. to thread bet. r.'s that were left for top. **2nd Shuttle**—Ch. of 20 d. s., r. of 10 d. s., p., 2 d. s., p., 2 d. s., p.. 10 d. s., close. Rep. around top, j. top rings by 1st p.

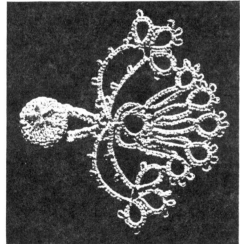

No 533—Frog

Make r. of 10 d. s., * p., 2 d. s., * 4 times, p., 10 d. s., close; ch. 12 d. s., fasten to 1st p. of r., ch. 8 d. s., 3 d. s., *p., 2 d. s., * 4 times, p., 3 d. s., close; ch. 8 d. s., fasten to same p. on r., fasten thread across to next p., 10 d. s., r. as before, j. to 1st r. by last p., ch. 10 d. s., fasten to same p., fasten thread to next p. of large r., ch. 12 d. s., r. as before; rep. ch. same length as 1st two; fasten to p. as before, ch. 12 d. s., fasten at beginning, *ch. 10 d. s., p. * 3 times, 10 d. s., clover leaf 3 rings of * 5 d. s., p. * 3 times, 5 d. s., fasten by inside p., *ch. 10 d. s., p. * 5 times, 10 d. s., fasten at beginning and rep. ch. and clover leaf an other side. Make ch. for loop over button with coarser thread, any length desired.

No 534—No. 30 Thread. Tatting Sewing Outfit.

Thimble Holder—R. 5 d. s., p., 5 d. s., p., 5 d. s., p., close. R. 5 d. s., j., 5 d. s., p., 5 d. s., p., 5 d. s., close. Rep. twice. Tie and cut. R. 5 d. s., p., 5 d. s., j. to previous square. 5 d. s., p., 5 d. s., close. R. 5 d. s., j., 5 d. s. j., 5 d. s., p., 5 d. s., close; rep. twice; tie and cut. Rep. until circle of 4 squares are made. **Bottom**—R. 5 d. s., p., 5 d. s., j. to circle; 5 d. s., p., 5 d. s., close. R. 5 d. s., j., 5 d. s., j. to circle, 5 d. s., p., 5 d. s., close. Rep. twice. **Top**—Ch. 3 d. s., 11 p. sep. by 2 d. s., 3 d. s., j. to circle Ch. 3 d. s., j. to previous scallop, 10 p. sep. by 2 d. s., 3 d. s., j. Rep. twice. **Rings**—R. 2 d. s., p., 2 d. s., p., 2 d. s., p., 2 d. s., close, j. to bone ring by pulling thread through rings and slipping shuttle through loop. R. 2 d. s., j., 2 d. s., p., 2 d. s., p., 2 d. s., close. Rep. until 21 rings are made on two top bone rings and 20 on each of other 3 R. 5 d. s., j. to top bone ring, 6 p. sep. by 2 d. s., 5 d. s., close, tn. R. 5 d. s., sk. 1 r., j., to next r., 6 p. sep. by 2 d. s., close, tn. R. 5 d. s., j. to previous r., 6 p. sep. by 2 d. s., close, tn. Rep. until 6 r.'s are made on each side, j. last 2 to 2nd bone ring, as at top. Tie and cut. R. 3 d. s., j. to 11th small r. on 2nd bone ring, 4 p. sep. by 2 d. s., 3 d. s., close, tn. R. 3 d. s., j. to 11th r. on other side, 4 p. sep. by 2 d. s., 3 d. s., close, tn. Rep. until 13 are made on each side, j. last 2 rings to another bone ring, tie and cut. R. 2 d. s., j. to 10th r. from top, 2 d. s., p., 2 d. s., p., 2 d. s., close, tn. R. 2 d. s., j. to 10th r. from top on other side, 2 d. s., p., 2 d. s., p., 2 d. s., close. Rep. until 3 are made on each side, j. 2 last ones to emery bag; tie and cut. R. 3 d. s., j. to 10th r. from top of 2nd bone ring, 4 p. sep. by 2 d. s., 3 d. s., close, tn. J. next r. to 9th r. from top; rep. until 23 r.'s are made on each side, j. to another bone ring; tie and cut. R. 2 d. s., j. to 10th r. from top, 2 d. s., p., 2 d. s., p., 2 d. s. close. Rep. until 3 are made on each side, tie and cut. Tie scissors to 1 p. only. R. 3 d. s., j. to 10th p. from top of 2nd bone ring on other side, 4 p. sep. by 2 d. s., 3 d. s., close, tn. R. 3 d. s., j. to 9th p., 4 p. sep. by 2 d. s., 3 d. s., close. Rep. until 5 are made on each side, j. to another bone ring, tie and cut. R. 2 d. s., j. to 10th r. from top, 2 d. s., p., 2 d. s., p., 2 d. s., close, tn. R. 2 d. s., j. to 10th row from top on other side, 2 d. s., p., 2 d. s., p., 2 d. s., close. Rep. until 5 are made on each side, j. last 2 to 1 scallop of thimble holder, tie and cut. Rep. ch. j. at top to same 2 r.'s, as previous ch.; j. at bottom to opp. scallop on thimble holder.

No 503

R. 3 d. s., p. 2 d. s., 7 times with p. bet. each, 2 d. s., 3 d. s., close. Make 2 more like last one, working close at base, ch. 4 d. s., until there are 4 groups of 4 d. s. with 3 p. bet. the pig, 3 d. s., j. 5 times, 4 d. s., close, ch. as before.

No. 505.

Make clover leaf of 3 r. of * 5 d. s., p. * 3 times, 5 d. s., j. by inside p. 2nd Shuttle—*ch. 10 d. s., p. * 3 times, 10 d. s., j. to 2nd p. of last r. of clover leaf, continue ch. of * 10 d. s., p. * 3 times, 10 d. s., now another clover leaf like 1st one, j. 1st p. of 1st r. of clover leaf to last p. on 1 ch., make 2nd ch. of *10 d. s., p. * 2 times, 10 d. s., j. to middle p. of 1st clover leaf. Continue ch. of *10 d. s., p. * 2 times, 10 d. s., j. to 2nd p. of last ring of last clover leaf. Continue ch. of *10 d. s., p. * 3 times, 10 d. s. Rep. to desired length.

No. 507

*R. 4 d. s., p., 4 d. s., * 3 times, close, ch. 2 d. s., 5 p. sep. by 2 d. s., draw up, r. 4 d. s., j. to last p. in 1st r., continue same as first. R. 4 d. s., j. to 1st p., 4 d. s., j. to p., 4 d. s., p., 4 d. s., close. Ch. as before, continue in this way to desired length. Then with shuttle thread, r. 4 d. s., p., 4 d. s., j. to center of last 2 r., 4 d. s., close. Ch. as before; r. as before, j. at center and last p., close. Rep. with another r., then ch. Continue this way until ready to join end as shown on illustration.

No 510

Make 2 rings, *5 d. s., p. * 3 times, 5 d. s., ch. 10 d. s., clover leaf of 3 rings, * 5 d. s., p. * 3 times, 5 d. s., fasten by inside p., ch. 10 d. s. Rep.

No. 520

R. 10 d. s., p., 5 d. s., p., close. 2nd Shuttle—Ch. 5 d. s., *p., 2 d. s., * 2 times, p. 5 d. s., p. 6 d. s., j. to 1st p. of ring, 6 d. s., *r., 5 d. s., p. * 3 times, 5 d. s., close; ch. 6 d. s., r. 10 d. s., p., 5 d. s., p., 5 d. s., ch., 6 d. s., j. to p. on ch. opp, 5 d. s., *p. 2 d. s., * 2 times, p., 5 d. s., p., 6 d. s., j. to preceding r.

No. 546.

R. *5 d. s., p. * 3 times, 5 d. s., close; ch. *5 d. s., p. * 4 times, 5 d. s., r. 10 d. s., j. to last p. of preceding r., 5 d. s., p., 5 d. s., close; ch. 6 d. s., r. 5 d. s., *p., 2 d. s., * 3 times, p., 5 d. s., close; ch. 6 d. s., r. 5 d. s., p., 5 d. s., p., 10 d. s., close; ch. 5 d. s., j. to p. opp., *5 d. s., p., * 3 times. 5 d. s. Rep.

No 551

Make r. of *5 d. s., p. * 3 times, 5 d. s., close; leave thread 1-8-inch, r. *3 d. s., p. * 3 times, 3 d. s., thread 1-8-inch, r. as at 1st, j. to 1st by side p., 1-8-inch thread, r. 5 d. s., j. to last p. on small r., 5 d. s., p., 2 d. s., p., 2 d. s., p., 5 d. s., p. 5 d. s., close; 1-8-inch thread, r. as 1st, j. to 2nd one like it, 1-8-inch thread, small r., j. to large, 1-8-inch thread; 4th r. as 1st. Rep. small r., only do not j. to preceding small r.

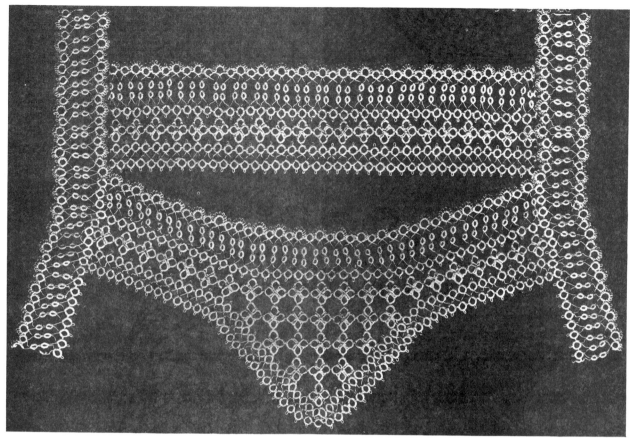

No. 542.

No. 50—Cotton—Make small suares of 4 rings, each ring for squares, 6 d. s., p., 6 d. s., p., 3 times, close. Make a row of 21 squares for front and back, both joined at corners; a row of 7 squares under center 7 of the 21 squares; a row of 5 squares; a row of 3 squares; a row of 1 square, joined together. Join below this a double row of rings of 5 d. s., p., 6 d. s., p., 6 d. s., p., 5 d. s., close, joined together.

Row at Top and Around Armholes—R. 5 d. s., p., 6 d. s., p., 6 d. s., p., 5 d. s., close; leave short thread; small ring of 7 d. s., p., 7 d. s., close; join by large rings in this row to top of every other square at top of yoke. Rep. this row for under side of armhole, under side of back and front of yoke. Make a double row joined to this by p. of small r. as follows† 7 d. s., j. to small ring of last r., 7 d. s., close; leave short thread, r. 5 d. s., p., 6 d. s., p., 6 d. s., p., 5 d. s., close; r. 4 d. s., j. 1st r. in this row, 10 p., 2 d., s. bet. 4 d. s., close. Rep. this double row around top of yoke and outside of armhole. Draw ribbon through bars.

No. 569—Cap.

Wheel in Center of Crown—*R. 2 d. s., p., 2 d. s., * twice, close, tn.; leave 1-8 in. thread, *r. 5 d. s., p., 5 d. s., * 3 times, close, tu.; leave 1-8 in. thread, r. 2 d. s., j. to 2nd p. of preceding small r., 2 d. s., p., 2 d. s., close, tn.; leave 1-8 in. thread, large r., j. by 1st p. to 3rd p. of preceding r.; rep., alternating small and large rings, j. as directed until you have 12 of each, j. last to 1st p. of both and fasten. **2nd Row**—Make a ch. of 6 d. s., joining by p. to p. of large r. of wheel, 2 rings, close together at the base, made of 6 d. s., p., 6 d. s., p., close. Pass shuttle under spool thread toward you and make a ch. j. to next r. of wheel, a r. j. to p. of last r., another r., close to this; rep. from, making 12 chs. and 12 groups of rings; j. last r. to p. of 1st r., tie chs. and cut thread. **3rd Row**—Make a r., j. to p., which connects 2 rings of last row, a ch., another r., j. to same p., a ch.; rep. around, j. last ch. at base of 1st r.; tie and cut thread. **4th Row**—Same as 2nd row, j. the p. of ch. to p. of ch. in 3rd row. **5th Row**—Same as 3rd, but j. only 1 r. to every alternate group, thus making 4 rings in one group, 3 in next, and so on. **6th Row**—Ch. 6 d. s., j. to p. of 1st ch. to right ch. of 6 d. s., a r., ch. 6 d. s., j. to p. of next ch. and continue same as 4th row around to within 1 ch. of starting pt., ending the row as begun; fasten. **7th Row**—Counting toward right of center, tie thread in p., j. 2nd group of rings, ch. 6 d. s., working the ends in, a r. j. to p. connecting next group of rings, and continue same as 3rd row until you reach the 2nd group of rings counting from center to left; cut and tie. **8th Row**—A r. j. to p. of ch. in 6th row, a ch., a r. j. to next p., rep. across front, 29 rings in all. Do not cut thread, but twist, leaving 1-2 in. **9th Row**—Same as 4th row and at end leave the 1-2 in. twisted thread. **10th Row**—Same as 3rd row. **11th Row**—Same as 8th row, except that the chs. are j. to p. of ch. in preceding row. At end pass both threads behind r. and j. to p. **12th Row**—Ch. 6 d. s., and continue like 4th row across front of cap. **13th Row**—Ch. 6 d. s. and continue across front same as in 3rd row, then work across bottom, making ch. of 6 d. s., p., 6 d. s., fastening at regular intervals; tie and cut thread.

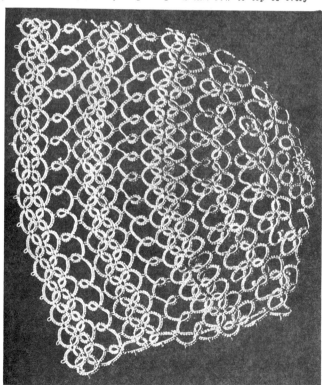

No. 556—Handkerchief.

R. 10 d. s., p., 5 d. s., p., 5 d. s., close; ch. 10 d. s., p., 2 d. s., p., 10 d. s., fasten to end p. of r. Rep. r. and ch. desired length.

No. 557—Handkerchief

Clover Leaf—R. 10 d. s., p., 5 d. s., p., 5 d. s., close; r. 5 d. s., j. to last p. of preceding row, 5 d. s., *p., 2 d. s., * 2 times, p., 5 d. s., close; r. as 1st, j. to last p. of middle r., ch. 5 d. s., p., 2 d. s., p., 5 d. s.; fasten to p. on last r., rep. ch., r. 10 d. s., fasten to p. on last r. of clover leaf, 5 d. s., *p., 1 d. s., * 2 times, p., 5 d. s., close. Rep. ch., then clover leaf.

No. 558—Handkerchief.

1st Row—R. 2 d. s., fasten to edge of kerchief, 2 d. s., close; leave 1-4th in. thread. Rep. r., rep. around handkerchief. **2nd Row**—Same as 1st, only j. r. by p. to middle of thread bet. r. of first row. **3rd Row**—J. r. as 2nd row, leave 1-8 in. thread, rep. r. with 2 d. s., p., 2 d. s.; leave 1-8 inch thread, make r. j. to preceding row.

No. 559—Handkerchief.

*R. 5 d. s., p., * 3 times, 5 d. s., ch. 5 d. s., p., 2 d. s., p., 5 d. s., r., 5 d. s., j. to last p. of preceding row. *5 d. s., p., * 2 times, 5 d. s.; close. Rep. ch. and r. desired length.

No. 565.

*R 5 d. s., p., * 3 times, close; ch. 5 d. s., p., 5 d. s. Make a 2nd r. like 1st j. to last p. of 1st r. Rep.

No. 568.

*R. 4 d. s., p., * 3 times, close; make a 2nd r. just like 1st, close. With colored thread, ch. 8 d. s., p., 8d. s., make a 3rd r. and j. 2nd p. to middle p. of 2nd r. Rep.

No. 567.

*R. 5 d. s., p, * 3 times, 5 d. s., close; leave 1-4th-in. thread, make a small r. of 5 d. s., p., 5 d. s., close, tn.; leave 1-4th in. thread as before; make a 2nd r. like 1st and j. to last p. of 1st r., tn.; leave sp. as before and make a large r. of 4 d. s., j. to p. of small r., *2 d. s., p., * 8 times, 4 d. s., close. Rep.

No. 514

R. 4 d. s., p., 4 d. s., close; ch. 4 d. s., p.,
4 d. s. until desired length, ch. back, 4 d. s., j. to
r., p., 4 d. s. until all p.'s are taken up; cut and
tie thread. R. 4 d. s., p., 4 d. s., p., 4 d. s., p.,
4 d. s., close. R. 4 d. s., j. to last p., r. 4 d. s.,
j. to 1st p. in ch., 4 d. s., p., 4 d. s., close. Continue until there are 4 r.'s j. as illustrated, then
cut thread and fasten end with needle and thread.
Continue until all p.'s in ch. are taken up. R. 5
d. s., j. to lower p. in group, 4 d. s., close. Ch. 2
d. s., p., 6 d. s. until there are 5 p. Rep.

No. 516

R. 2 d. s. 8 times with p. bet. each 2 d. s.,
close; ch. 5 d. s., p., 9 d. s., p. 3 times with p. bet.
each 2 d. s., 9 d. s., p., 5 d. s., draw up, r. 2 d. s.
4 times, j. to 4th p. of last r., 2 d. s. 4 times with
p. bet. each 2 d. s., close; ch. 4 d. s., p., 4 d. s.,
draw up, r. as before, close. Continue this way
until desired width, then ch. 4 d. s., p., 4 d. s.,
finish end with 3-leaf clover, same as other r. was
made. Ch. 4 d. s., j. to last p. in ch., 4 d. s., r.
Rep. as before.

No. 522.

R. 5 d. s., *p., 2 d. s., * 4 times, p., 5 d. s.,
close. 2nd Shuttle—Ch. 10 d. s., *p, 2 d. s., * 2
times, p., 10 d. s., r. 5 d. s., p., 10 d. s., p., 5
d. s., close; ch. 10 d. s., r. 5 d. s., j. to r. just
made, 10 d. s., p., 5 d. s., close. On opp. side
make 2 r. of 5 d. s., *p., 2 d. s., * 4 times, p.,
5 d. s. each, close; ch. 10 d. s., r. 5 d. s., j. to inside
r., 10 d. s., p., 5 d. s., close; r. on outside of 5
d. s., *p., 2 d. s., * 4 times p., 5 d. s., close; ch.
10 d. s., clover leaf of 3 rings, 5 d. s., j. to outside r. above, *2 d. s., p. * 4 times, 5 d. s., close.
Make 3 such rings j. at 1st p., ch. 10 d. s., inside
r. like other inside rings, outside r. same as other
outside rings joined to clover leaf, ch. 10 d. s.,
inside r., 2 outside rings, ch. 10 d. s., inside r.
joined to 1st inside r. made. Rep. 1 ch., make 2
rings like outside rings, j. by inside p. and j.
to nearest outside r. of pt. to 1st p. on outside
r. and next to last p. of rings bet. pt.

No. 550

R. *5 d. s., p., * 3 times, 5 d. s.; leave thread
1 inch, then r. joined by side p., make desired
length, then make r. 2 d. s., j. to middle of long
thread left bet. r., 2 d. s., close; leave long thread
as in 1st row, rep .r. Rep. rows until edge is of
desired length.

No. 554

Make clover leaf of 3 rings, 5 d. s., *p., 2
d. s., * 13 times, p., 5 d. s., j. by 1st inside p., ch.
9 d. s., *p., 2 d. s., * 2 times, p., 4 d., s., r., *2
d. s., p., * 2 times, 2 d. s., j. to 4th p. in 1st r.
of clover leaf, *2 d. s., p. 2 times, 2 d. s., close;
rep., ch. and r. around clover leaf, making 4 r.
to each of 3 r. of clover leaf with ch. bet., fastening middle p. of r. to every other p. on clover leaf,
skipping 1st 4 ch. Rep. 1st 1 ch., fasten at beginning. Make medallions to form desired length
and j. by r., 4 d. s., p., 4 d. s., j. to middle p.
of 2nd ch. of medallion, 4 d. s., p., 4 d. s., close;
ch. 4 d. s., *p., 2 d. s., * 3 times, p., 4 d. s., j. to
middle p. of top ch. of medallion. Rep. ch. 3 times
to each medallion then r. as at first.

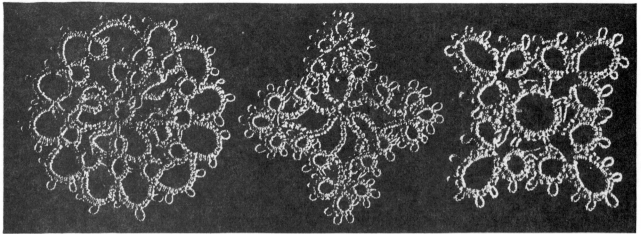

..No. 527—*R. 2 d. s., p. * 8 times, close, cut and tie, r. 5 d. s., j. to p., 5 d. s., close; ch. 6 d. s., j. to to p., 6 d. s., draw up. Rep. until there are 4 r. and 4 ch., caught to center rings, tie and cut, *r., 4 d. s., p., 4 d. s., * 3 times, close; ch. 4 d. s., p., 4 d. s., p., 4 d. s., draw up. R. as before until there are 12 rings and chains each. Rep.

No. 528—R. 2 d. s., p. until there are 5 p., then 2 d. s., close. Make 3 rings like 1st one, j. at 1st p., draw together in three-leaf clover. 2nd Shuttle—5 d. s., r. like 1st, but j. 2nd p. to 3rd r. in clover leaf, close; ch. 5 d. s., large p., 5 d. s., r. like last one, j. both at 2nd p., ch. 5 d. s., r. 3 d. s., clover leaf as 1st, then ch. 5, r. as before; ch. 5 d. s., j. to p., 5 d. s., continue in this way until all is made.

No 529—Large r., 4 d. s., p., *2 d. s., p., * 4 times, 4 d. s., close r, 2 d. s., p., j. to p. of center r., *2 d. s., p. * 4 times, close r, 4 d. s., j. to last p. of r. just made, *2 d. s., p., * 6 times, 4 d. s., close r. 2 d. s., j. to last p. of large r., *2 d. s., p. * 4 times, close, j. last p. to 2nd p. of center r. Rep. this clover leaf three times to form the 4 corners of the med.

No. 512 (2 Shuttles)—Commence with small r. of clover leaf, 2 d. s., *1 p., 1 d. s., * 5 times, close; 2 d. s., j. to last p. of r., *1 p., 1 d. s., * 5 times, p., close; close large r., 2 d. s., j. to last p. of large r., *1 d. s., 1 p., * 4 times, 2 d. s., close. 2nd Shuttle—6 d. s., *1 p., 1 d. s., * 4 times, draw up smooth and even. 1st Shuttle—2 d. s., *1 p., 1 d. s., * 3 times, 2 d. s., close. 2nd Shuttle—*1 d. s., p., * 4 times, 6 d. s., draw up smooth and even. Rep. from beginning of clover leaf.

No. 525—6 d. s., p., *2 d. s., p., * 4 times, 6 d. s., close; 6 d. s., j. to last p. of 1st petal, *2 d. s., p., * 2 times, 6 d. s., close. Alternate, making 3 like 1st and 4 like 2nd, until you have 8—four large petals and 4 small ones.

No. 538—Fancy Square Medallion (Two Shuttles—R. 10 d. s., tn., ch. 10 d. s., 3 p., sep. by 3 d. s. Shuttle No 2—R. 7 p., sep. by 2 d. s., close. Shuttle No. 1—Ch. 3 p., sep. by 3 d. s., 10 d. s., j. in r. ch. 10 d. s. Shuttle No 2—R. 7 p., sep. by 2 d. s., close. Shuttle No. 1—Ch. 10 d. s., p., tn., 15 d. s., j. to last p. of r., tn., ch. 3 d. s., 5 p., sep. by 2 d. s., 3 d. s., j. in p. on ch., 3 d. s., 5 p., sep. by 2 d. s., 3 d. s., p., tn., ch. 15 d. s., j. in p. on ch., tn., ch 10 d. s. Shuttle No. 2—R. 7 p., sep. by 2 d. s., close. Shuttle No 1—Ch. 10 d. s., j., rep. around.

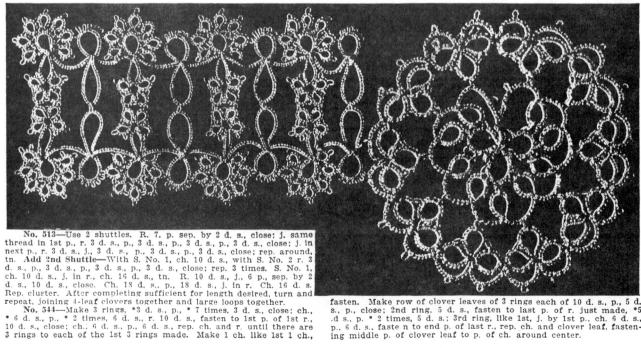

No. 513—Use 2 shuttles. R. 7. p. sep. by 2 d. s., close; j. same thread in 1st p., r. 3 d. s., p., 3 d. s., p., 3 d. s., p., 3 d. s., close; j. in next p., r. 3 d. s., j., 3 d. s., p., 3 d. s., p., 3 d. s., close; rep. around, tn. Add 2nd Shuttle—With S. No. 1, ch. 10 d. s., with S. No. 2 r. 3 d. s., p., 3 d. s., p., 3 d. s., p., 3 d. s., close; rep. 3 times. S. No. 1, ch. 10 d. s., j. in r., ch. 16 d. s., tn. R. 10 d. s., j. in p. on ch., 3 d. s., 10 d. s., close. Ch. 18 d. s., j. in r. Ch. 16 d. s. Rep. cluster. After completing sufficient for length desired, turn and repeat, joining 4-leaf clovers together and large loops together.

No. 544—Make 3 rings, *3 d. s., p., * 7 times, 3 d. s., close; ch., * 6 d. s., p. * 2 times, 6 d. s., r. 10 d. s., fasten to 1st p. of 1st r., 10 d. s., close; ch., 6 d. s., p., 6 d. s., rep. ch. and r. until there are 3 rings to each of the 1st 3 rings made. Make 1 ch. like 1st 1 ch.,

fasten. Make row of clover leaves of 3 rings each of 10 d. s., p., 5 d. s., p., close; 2nd ring, 5 d. s., fasten to last p. of r. just made, *5 d. s., p. * 2 times, 5 d. s.; 3rd ring, like 1st, j. by 1st p., ch. 6 d. s., p., 6 d. s., fasten to end p. of last r., rep. ch. and clover leaf, fastening middle p. of clover leaf to p. of ch. around center.

No. 506

R. 5 d. s., p. 10 d. s., p., 5 d. s., close. **2nd Shuttle**—*ch., 3 d. s., p. * 3 times, 3 d. s. until there are 7 r. j. p. and 6 ch. Make 1 ch. of 10 d. s., *p., 2 d. s., * 3 times, p., 10 d. s., r. 10 d. s., j. to 2nd p. of last ch. bet. r. in wheel, 5 d. s., p., 5 d. s., close; r. 5 d. s., j. to p. of preceding r., *5 d. s., p. * 2 times, 5 d. s., close; r. 5 d. s., j. to last p. of preceding r., 5 d. s., p., 10 d. s., close. This forms a clover leaf bet. each wheel. Rep. 1 ch., then wheel.

No 519.

Form r. of 10 d. s., p., 10 d. s., close; fasten 2nd shuttle thread and make ch. of 5 d. s., p., 2 d. s., p., 2 d. s., p., 5 d. s.; with 1st shuttle thread make r. like 1st, only j. center of r. to p. of 1st r.; rep. until there is a wheel of 6 r. with 6 ch. bet.; with both shuttles make ch. of *6 d. s., p. * 3 times, *2 d. s., p. * 2 times, *6 d. s., p. * 2 times, 6 d. s., make r. of 10 d. s., j. to middle p. of last ch. of wheel, 10 d. s., close; ch. 6 d. s., clover leaf of 3 r. of *5 d. s., p. * 3 times, 5 d. s., j. by inside p., ch. of 6 d. s., r. of 10 d. s., p., 10 d. s., ch. 6 d. s., fasten to p. on opp. ch., *6 d. s., p. * 2 times, *2 d. s., p. * 2 times, *6 d. s., p. * 2 times, 6 d. s. Begin wheel as at first and rep. to desired length.

No. 524

Make r. of 3 p. with 5 d. s. bet., close. Make 2nd r. 5 d. s., j. to last p. of r. just made, 5 d. s., *p., 2 d. s., * 2 times, p., 5 d. s., close. Make 3rd r. like 1st and j. 1st p. to last p. of 2nd r. Draw together closely at base to form clover leaf. **2nd Shuttle**—*ch. 6 d. s., p. * 4 times, 6 d. s. **1st Shuttle**—Leave thread 1-4-inch long and make r. of 6 p. with 2 d. s. bet., close. **2nd Shuttle**—Ch. 6 d. s., fasten to p., make ch. bet. each p. Make 1st st. of each ch. loose so as to fasten 2nd ch. by pulling thread through with crochet hook. Make 2nd row of ch. of 8 d. s. each; 3rd row, 10 d. s. each; 4th row, *2 d. s., p. * 5 times, 2 d. s. When last ch. is made fasten closely to 1 ch. when fastening to preceding row. Then, with 2nd shuttle, rep. 1 ch.

..No. 560.

Make clover leaf of 3 rings of *5 d. s., p. * 3 times, 5d. s., j. by inside p., *ch. 5 d. s., p. * 3 times, 5d. s., r. 10 d. s., p., 10 d. s., ch. 10 d. s., j. to p. on last r. of clover leav, 10 d. s., r. as before, j. to last r. by p., ch. 5 d. s., *p., 2 d. s., * 2 times, p., 5 d. s., clover leaf of 3 r. as at first. Rep. last ch., also inside r., ch. 10 d. s., p., 10 d. s., rep. r., rep. top ch.

No. 564

R. 10 d. s., p., 5 d. s., p., 5 d. s., close; r. 5 d. s., j. to last p. on r. before *3 d. s., p. * 3 times, 3 d. s., p., 5 d. s., r. like 1st, j. by 1st p. to last p. on preceding r., ch. *5 d. s., p., * 6 times, 5 d. s., r. *5 d. s., p. * 3 times, 5 d. s., close; ch. *5 d. s., p. * 3 times, 5 d. s., r. like one just before, j. by middle p. to middle p. of one before; rep. ch., rep. r., then tn. work and make r. on outside, 5 d. s., j. to last p. of last ch., 5 d. s., p., *3 d. s., p. * 2 times, 5 d. s., p., 5 d. s., close. Now make r. on inside as before, j. to preceding inside r. by 1st p., rep. ch., j. 1st p. to last p. of outside r., rep. inside r., j. to last one by middle p., rep. ch., rep. r., j. as before, j. last r. to first r. by last p. Rep. 1 ch.

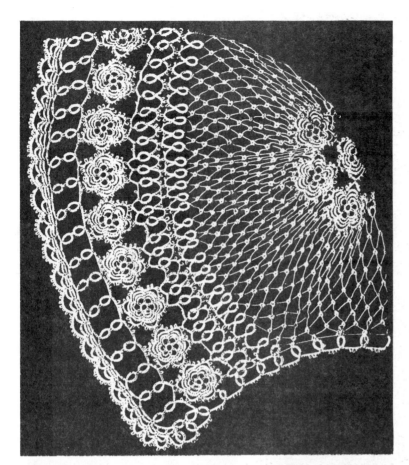

No. 543—Cap.

The center of the back is formed by 7 roses made as follows: R. 1 d. s., *p., 2 d. s., * 5 times, p., 1 d. s., close; ch. 6 d. s., bet. each p. on r. or 6 ch.; make 1st st. of ch. loose so next ch. of 8 d. s. can be fastened at same place; 3rd row, ch. 10 d. s.; 4th row, *2 d. s., p. * 5 times, ,2 d. s. These roses are fastened by middle p. of last ch. on 3 sides.

Net Work is formed by r. of 2 d. s. fastened to every other p. on outer edge of roses, 2 d. s., close and leave thread 1-2 in. long bet. small rings. 2nd row of small ring are fastened to middle of 1-2in. thread bet. rings. Rep. to desired size. The next row is made of r. 10 d. s. fastened to thread bet. small rings, 10 d. s., close; ch. 5 d. s., *p., 2 d. s., * 2 times, p., 5 d. s. Rep. around, leaving about 4 inches for back of cap. Next row is made the same, only joined by ch. Ch. 5 d. s., p., 2 d. s., j. to middle p. of last ch., 2 d. s., p., 5 d. s., r. 10 d. s., p. 10 d. s. Rep. length of last row. Row of ch. of 5 d. s., p., 5 d. s. bet. each r. fastened to p. of r. Row of roses same as back fastened to ch. of middle p. of outside petal of rose to p. of ch. Fasten two petals, leaving 1 p. on ch. free bet. each rose. Fasten roses together by end petals leaving two petals for outside edge. Next row, ch. 5 d. s., p., 2 d. s. fasten to middle p. on petal of rose, 2 d. s., p., 5 d. s., r. 10 d. s. Next row same joining by p. on r., ch. 5 d. s., p., 5 d. s., p., 5 d. s.

Outside Edge—Ch. 6 d. s. for 1st row fastened to p. on ch. **2nd Row**—8 d. s., fastened where 1st row is fastened. **3rd Row**—10 d. s., fastened where 2nd row is fastened. **4th Row**—*2 d. s., p., * 7 times, 2 d. s., fasten where every other ch. of last row is fastened.

Edge to tail is made of r. 10 d. s., fastened to edge of cap, 10 d. s., close; ch. 5 d. s., *p., 2 d. s., * 2 times, 5 d. s.

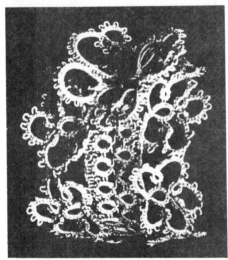

No. 536---No. 30 Thread Napkin Ring.

Make band as instructions for No. 535 Handle, until 24 r.'s are made on each side; tie and cut. Ch. 3 d. s., p., 2 d. s., j. to band, 2 d. s., p., 2 d. s., p., 2 d. s., j., 2 d. s., p. 2 d. s., p., 2 d. s., j., 2 d. s., tn. Make floral design as No. 535, Basket; tn., ch. 3 d. s., p., 2 d. s., sk. one r.on band, j. to next r., 2 d. s., p., 2 d. s., p., 2 d. s., j., 2 d. s., p., 2 d. s., p., 2 d. s., j., 2 d. s., p., 3 d. s., tn. Rep. around, tie and cut. Rep. on other side of band. **Butterfly** same as on No. 535, Basket. Stiffening process same as for No. 535, Basket.

No. 541—Centerpiece. Use 50 or 60 Crochet Cotton. Insertion.

*R 4 d. s., p. * 3 times, close, tn.; leave 1-4 in. thread, *r. 5 d. s., p. * 3 times, close, tn.; leave 1-4 in. thread, r. 4 d. s., j. to side p. of 1st small r., * 4 d. s., p. * 2 times, tn. Rep. to desired length. Sew on side of small rings to linen.

Medallion—Make a *r of 1 d. s., 1 l. p., * 17 times, close and fasten securely. Make a r. of 6 d. s., j. to p. of 1st r. made ,6 d. s., close, tn. your work, leave 1-4 in. thread, make a r. of 4 d. s., p.,

1 d. s., p., 6 times, making 7 p. in all, 4 d. s., close. Turn your work and repeat; j. the outside rings by first and last p., continue around until wheel is finished. Join three wheels with needle and thread, then join to insertion on linen center. The number of wheels needed will depend on size of linen center.

No. 511—Two Shuttles.

3 d. s., p., *1 d. s., p., * 4 times, 3 d. s.; draw up to form r. 2nd Shuttle—10 d. s., draw up even and smooth, with 1st shuttle make another r. as the 1st was made, 3 d. s., p., *1 d. s., p., * 3 d. s. With 2nd shuttle make 10 d. s., followed by another r., 3 d. s., and j. to 1st p. of 1st r.

No. 515.

Make wheel of 6. r. of 10 d. s., p. 10 d. s., fasten all 6 together with p., make ch. bet. each r. of 5 d. s., p., * 2 d. s., p. * twice, 5 d. s. After wheel is complete, make a ch. with 2nd shuttle of * 6 d. s., p., * 5 times, 6 d. s., make r. of 10 d. s., fasten to 1st p. of next to last ch. of wheel, 5 d. s., p., 5 d. s., close, ch. of 6 d. s., wheel like 1st, fasten 2nd p. of 1st ch. to p. of r. above, ch. of 6 d. s., r. of 5 d. s., fasten to middle p. of last ch. of wheel, 5 d. s., p., 10 d. s., ch. of 6 d. s., fasten to p. opp. on long ch., * 6 d. s., p., * 4 times, 6 d. s., rep. to desired length.

No. 517.

*R. 5 d. s., p., * 3 times, 5 d. s., close. 2nd Shuttle—*Ch. 3 d. s., p., * 3 times 3 d. s., r. 5 d. s., j. to last p. of preceding r., *5 d. s., p., * 2 times, 5 d. s., close, rep. ch. and r. until there are 7 rings, j. last r. to 1st p. of 1st r., making 6 ch. bet. the 7 rings, * ch. 6 d. s., p. * 3 times, 6 d. s. fasten to middle p. of last ch. made bet. rings. Ch. of 6 d. s., rep. 1st scallop of 7 rings, 6 ch. bet., ch. 6 d. s., p. on opp. side of ch. made by turning ch. until p. is formed then turning back and making ch. of 6 d. s., make r. of 5 d. s., p., 5 d. s., fasten to p. opp. on 1 ch., 5 d. s., p., 5 d. s., close, * ch. 6 d. s., p. * 3 times, 6 d. s. Rep. from first to desired length.

No. 552.

Make r. of 6 d. s., *p., 2 d. s., * 4 times, 6 d. s., close. 2nd Shuttle—Ch. 10 d. s., p., 10 d. s., fasten to 1st p. of r., ch. 8 d. s., r. *3 d .s., p., * 3 times, 3 d. s., close; ch. 8 d. s., fasten to same 1st p., fasten thread across to next p. of 1st r., ch. 9 d. s., r. as before, ch. 9 d. s., fasten in same p., fasten across to 3rd p., ch. 10 d. s., r., ch. 10 d. s. fasten as before and rep. ch. of 9 d. s., also of 8 d. s. with rings as before. These rings are fastened by side p., ch. 10 d. s., p., 10 d. s., fasten to top of 1st r., ch. 8 d. s., p., 5 d. s., p., 5 d. s., r. *5 d. s., p., * 3 times, 5 d. s., close.
Edge—Ch. 5 d. s., p., 1 d. s., p., 5 d. s., bet. each p. of rings on edge.

No. 553.

R. 6 d. s., p., 4 d. s., p., 6 d. s., close. 2nd Shutttle—Ch. *3 d. s., p., * 5 times, 3 d. s., r. as before, j. by 1st p., ch. * 3 d. s., p., * 7 times, 3 d. s., r., ch. * 3 d. s., p., * 9 times, 3 d. s., r., ch. *3 d. s., p., * 7 times, 3 d. s., r. ch. * 3 d. s., p., * 5 times, 3 d. s., fasten at beginning, ch. * 6 d. s., p., * 6 times, 3 d. s., r., 6 d. s., fasten to middle p. on ch. having 7 p. on pansy, *2 d. s., p., * 5 times, 6 d. s., close. Rep. 1 ch., also r., 1 ch., then pansy.

No. 535—No. 30 Thread. Bon-Bon Basket.

Bottom—R. 7 d. s., 5 p. sep. by 2 d. s., 7 d. s., close. R. 7 d. s., j., 4 p. sep. by 2 d. s., 7 d. s., close. Rep. until 7 r.'s are made,, tie and cut. R. 2 d. s., p., 2 d. s., j. to center p. on on eof r.'s, 2 d. s., p., 2 d. s., close, tn. R. 5 d. s., p., 5 d. s., p., 2 d. s., p., 2 d. s., p., 5 d. s., p., 5 d. s., close, tn. R. 2 d. s., j. to 1st small r., 2 d. s., p., 2 d. s., p., 2 d. s., close, tn. Rep. large r., j. to 1st p., j. every 3rd small r. to centerwheel. Rep. around, tie and cut. R. 5 d. s., p., 5 d. s., p., 2 d. s., j. to bottom, 2 d. s., p., 5 d. s., p., 5 d. s., close, tn. R 4 d. s., p., 4 d. s., p., 2 d. s., p., 2 d. s., p., 4 d. s., 4 d. s., close. Rep. around j. to side of each r., tie and cut. With 2 shuttles, ch. 10 d. s., j.; shuttle No. 2, ch. 10 d. s.; shuttle No. 1, ch. l. p., 10 d. s., j. Rep. around tie and cut; ch. 3 d. s., j., 3 p., sep. by 2 d. s., j, 3 p. sep. by 2 d. s., j., 3 d. s., tn. **Floral Design** —R. 4 d. s., p., 4 d. s., p., 4 d. s., p., 4 d. s., close. Ch. 3 d. s., 5 p. sep. by 2 d. s., 3 d. s., tn. R 4 d. s., j. to 1st p. on r., 4 d. s., close. Rep. ch. and r.'s, j. to r.'s in top p. of center r., tn. Ch. 3 d. s., p., 2 d. s., j., 5 p. sep. by 2 d. s., j., 2 d. s., p., 3 d. s., tn. Rep. design and j. 2nd ch. to center p. of 4th ch. on last design, rep. around. **Handle**—R. 3 d. s., j. 1st p. at top of floral design, 4 p. sep. by 2 d. s., 3 d. s., close, tn. R. 3 d. s., j. to last p. on floral design, 4 p. sep. by 2 d. s., 3 d. s., close, tn. Rep. r.'s, j. by 1st and last p. until 22are made on each side, j. end ones to floral design just opp. **Butterfly**—R. 3 p. sep. by 2 d. s., 2 large p., 3 p. sep. by 2 d. s., close. R. 3 p. sep. by 3 d. s., medium p., 3 p. sep. by 2 d. s., close, tie and cut. **Large Wing**—J. both threads to center p. of top of body, ch. 2 d. s. j. to top, 5 p. sep. by 2 d. s., tn. R 2 d. s., p., 2 d. s., p., 2 d. s., p., 2 d. s., close, tn. Ch. 5 p. sep. by 2 d. s., tn. R. 2 d. s., j., 2 d. s., p., 2 d. s., p., 2 d. s., close, tn. Ch. 13 p. sep. by 2 d. s., j. to last p. on top of body, 2 d. s., tie

and cut. **Small Wing**—J. to center p. of lower body, r. 3 d. s., j. to top p., 3 d. s., j. to 2nd p. on large wing, 2 d. s., j 2 d. s., j., 12 p. sep. by 2 d. s., j. to bottom p., 3 d. s., tie and cut. Tie butterfly to handle. For stiffening basket, pour boiling water over an equal amount of sugar, stir until clear and dip. Put on mold until partly dry and shape with fingers.

No. 540—Butterfly Medallion—No. 30 Thread

Head—R. 8 d. s., p., 1 d. s., close; r. 1 d. s., j., 7 d. s., p., 1 d. s., close; r. 1 d. s., j., 8 d. s., close. **Top Body**—R 7 p., sep. by 4 d. s., close. R. 7 d. s., j. in middle p., 7 d. s., close; tie and cut. **Lower Body**—R. 6 p., sep. by 4 d. s., j. to top body, 6 p. sep. by 4 d. s., close. R. 10 d. s., large p., 10 d. s., close. R 18 d. s., j. to top body, 18 d. s., close. R. 16 d. s., j. to top body, 16 d. s., close, tie and cut. **Small Wing**—R 7 p. sep. by 3 d. s.; close. R. 3 d. s., p., 3 d. s., j. to 2nd p. from bottom, 3 d. s., p., 3 d. s., close; j. to large r. Rep. around. **Large Wing** —R. 9 p. sep. by 3 d. s., close. R 18 p., sep. by 3 d. s.; close. R. 3 d. s., p., 3 d. s., j. in middle p. of top body, 3 d. s., p., 3 d. s.; close. Rep. 3 times. R. 3 d. s., j., 6 p. sep. by 3 d. s.; close. Rep. 5 times. Rep. small rings 4 times, j. 1st and 2nd to small wing, 3rd to lower body, 4th to upper body, tie and cut. J. double thread to 1st large r. Ch. 4 p. sep. by 3 d. s., tn. R. 4 d. s., p., 4 d. s., j. to 2nd large r. at top, 4 d. s., p., 4 d. s., close. Rep. ch. R. 3 d. s., p., 3 d. s., p., 3 d. s., p., 3 d. s., close. Rep. ch. R. 4 d. s., p., 4 d. s., j. to 3rd large r., 4 d. s., p., 4 d. s., close. Rep. ch. R. 3 d. s., p., 3 d. s., j. to 4th large r., 3 d. s., p., 3 d. s., close. Rep. ch., j. to 5th large r.; tie and cut. **Feelers**—Ch. 10 d. s., j. to 1st p. on wing, 20 d. s., j. 15 d. s., j. to head on each side. 15 d. s., j., 20 d. s., j. to other wing, 10 d. s., tie and cut.

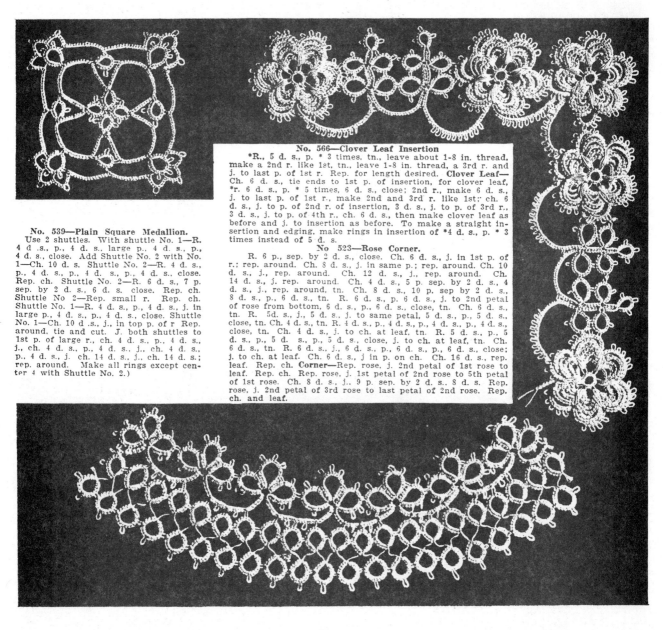

No. 539—Plain Square Medallion.

Use 2 shuttles. With shuttle No. 1—R. 4 d .s., p., 4 d. s. large p., 4 d. s., p., 4 d. s., close. Add Shuttle No. 2 with No. 1—Ch. 10 d. s. Shuttle No. 2—R. 4 d. s., p., 4 d. s., p., 4 d. s., p., 4 d. s., close. Rep. ch. Shuttle No. 2—R. 6 d. s., 7 p. sep. by 2 d. s., 6 d. s. close. Rep. ch. Shuttle No 2—Rep. small r. Rep. ch. Shuttle No. 1—R. 4 d. s., p., 4 d. s., j. in large p., 4 d. s., p., 4 d. s., close. Shuttle No. 1—Ch. 10 d. s., j., in top p. of r Rep. around, tie and cut. J. both shuttles to 1st p. of large r., ch. 4 d. s., p., 4 d. s., j., ch. 4 d. s., p., 4 d. s., j., ch. 4 d. s. p., 4 d. s., j. ch. 14 d. s., j.. ch. 14 d. s.; rep. around. Make all rings except center 4 with Shuttle No. 2.)

No. 566—Clover Leaf Insertion

*R., 5 d. s., p. * 3 times. tn., leave about 1-8 in. thread. make a 2nd r. like 1st, tn., leave 1-8 in. thread, a 3rd r. and j. to last p. of 1st r. Rep. for length desired. **Clover Leaf**— Ch. 6 d. s., tie ends to 1st p. of insertion, for clover leaf, *r. 6 d. s., p. * 5 times, 6 d. s., close; 2nd r., make 6 d. s., j. to last p. of 1st r., make 2nd and 3rd r. like 1st;· 6 d. s., j. to p. of 2nd r. of insertion, 3 d. s., j. to p. of 3rd r., 3 d. s., j. to p. of 4th r.. ch. 6 d. s., then make clover leaf as before and j. to insertion as before. To make a straight insertion and edging. make rings in insertion of *4 d. s., p. * 3 times instead of 5 d. s.

No 523—Rose Corner.

R. 6 p., sep. by 2 d. s., close. Ch. 6 d. s., j. in 1st p. of r.; rep. around. Ch. 8 d. s., j. in same p.; rep. around. Ch. 10 d. s., j., rep. around. Ch. 12 d. s., j. rep. around. Ch. 14 d. s., j. rep. around. Ch. 4 d. s., 5 p. sep. by 2 d. s., 4 d. s., j., rep. around, tn. Ch. 8 d. s., 10 d. s. sep by 2 d. s., 8 d. s., p., 6 d. s., tn. R. 6 d. s., p., 6 d. s., j. to 2nd petal of rose from bottom, 6 d. s., p., 6 d. s., close, tn. Ch. 6 d. s., tn. R. 5d. s., j., 5 d. s., j. to same petal, 5 d. s., p., 5 d. s., close, tn. Ch. 4 d. s., tn. R. 4 d. s., p., 4 d. s., j. to ch. at leaf, tn. R. 5 d. s., p., 5 d. s., p., 5 d. s., p., 5 d. s., close, j. to ch. at leaf, tn. Ch. 6 d. s., tn. R. 5 d. s., p., 5 d. s., p., 5 d. s., close, j. to ch. at leaf, tn. Ch. 6 d. s., tn. R. 6 d. s., j., 6 d. s., p., 6 d. s., p., 6 d. s., close; j. to ch. at leaf. Ch. 6 d. s., j in p. on ch. Ch. 16 d. s., rep. leaf. Rep. ch. **Corner**—Rep. rose, j. 2nd petal of 1st rose to leaf. Rep. ch. Rep. rose, j. 1st petal of 2nd rose to 5th petal of 1st rose. Ch. 8 d. s., j., 9 p. sep. by 2 d. s., 8 d. s. Rep. rose, j. 2nd petal of 3rd rose to last petal of 2nd rose. Rep. ch. and leaf.

BOOK ON NEW AND ORIGINAL DESIGNS IN TATTING

by
Marie
Antoinette
Hees

Book No. 05.

E.C. Spuehler
Publisher
SAINT LOUIS, MO.

R of 4 ds-p-2 ds-p-1 ds-p-1 ds-p-2 ds-p-4 ds-close-allow about ¼ inch thread-4 ds-join to last p-2 ds-p-1

No. 1

ds-p-1 ds-p-2 ds-p-4 ds-close and repeat to end.

R of 3 ds-p-3 ds-p-1 ds-p-1 ds-p-3 ds-p-3 ds-close *
ch 4 ds-p-1 ds-p-1 ds-p-4 ds-r-3 ds-join to last p of

No. 2

1st r-3 ds-p-1 ds-p-1 ds-p-3 ds-p-3 ds-close and repeat from * to end.

No. 10—Use 2 threads, wind shuttle without cutting thread; large r-2 ds-9 p-separated by 2 ds-ending with 2 ds-close-ch-7 ds-p-7 ds-r-2 ds-join to last p of large

No. 3

length-make another piece-joining ch to ch on first piece length-make another piece-joining ch to ch on first piece.

Ring of 5 ds-p-5 ds-close ch 4 ds-p-1 ds-p-4 ds-ring of 2 ds-5 p separated by 2 ds ending with 2 ds-close-ch 5 ds-r of 5 p separated by 2 ds-close-ch 5-join to last p of first ch-ch-4 ds-p-1 ds-p-4 ds-r of 5-join to center p of last ring made-5 ds-close-ch 4 ds-p-1 ds-p-4

No. 4

ds-p-4 ds-r of 2 ds-p-2 ds-p-2 ds-join to same p where small r was joined-2 ds-p-2 ds-p-2 ds-close-ch 2 ds-p-2 ds-r of 5 p separated by 2 ds-close-repeat last 3 times-ch 4 ds-join to last p of ch-ch 4 ds-p-1 ds-p-4 ds-repeat from beginning to length required.

No. 5

Same as edge on collar No. 26.

R of 12—p separated by 2 ds ending with 3 ds-r of 5 ds-join to 3rd p of 1st r-5 ds-close-ch 3 ds-5 p separated by 3 ds-3 ds-r of 5 ds-join to next p of 1st r-5 ds-

No. 6

close-ch 3 ds-p 3-p separated by 3 ds-3 ds-join to 7th p of 1st r made-ch 3 ds-3 p separated by 3 ds-3 ds-repeat-joining scallops together by center p of side ch.

No. 7

Same as wide handkerchief edge No. 23.

No. 8

Same as medallion on dresser scarf.

Tatted edge with novelty braid—Fasten thread in 3rd p-on 2nd loop of braid-ch 8-ds-join to 3rd p of 3rd loop of braid-5 ds-p-8 ds-join to 4th loop of braid-ch 8 ds-1 long p- 8 ds-join to 6th loop of braid-5 ds-p-5 ds-join to 7th loop of braid-ch 8 ds-join to 8th and 13th loop of 2nd piece of braid-turn-ch 8 ds-join to 10th loop

No. 9

No. 11

p as shown in illustration-ch of 7 ds-sk 1 pr on straight braid-join in next 7 ds-r of 8 ds-joining around cord on braid-8 ds-close-ch 4 ds-sk 1 pr-join in next 4 ds-make another r same as last-joining the two ps together-repeat from * to end.

of braid 8 ds-join to long p of 3rd ch on 1st row-ch 8 ds-join to 8th loop of braid-8 ds-join in same long p-ch 8 ds-join to 6th loop of braid-ch 8 ds-join to p of 2nd ch on 1st row-ch 8 ds-join to 4th loop of braid-ch 8 ds-join in ch where work was begun-sk-two loops of 1st piece of braid-join threads to 3rd loop and repeat-join between scallops with needle and thread-edge-r-4 ds-p-4 ds-join 1st loop of lower piece of braid- 4 ds-p-4 ds-turn * ch 4 ds-p-2 ds-repeat 3 times ending with 4 ds-turn-r of 4 ds-join to last p of 1st loop-4 ds-join to next loop of braid-4 ds-p-4 ds-repeat from * 9 times-then leave ch out-make 12th r-4 ds-p-4 ds-sk-two rings of braid-join to next loop 4 ds-p-4 ds-repeat.
Top-R of 4 ds-p-4 ds-join to 1st loop of 1st piece of braid-4 ds-p-4 ds-turn-r of 4 ds-p-4 ds-repeat 3 times-turn * r of 4 ds-join last p of 1st loop-4 ds-join to next loop of braid 4 ds-p-4 ds-turn-r of 4 ds-join last p of 2nd loop-4 ds-p-4 ds-repeat last twice then repeat from *.

R of 7 ps separated by 2 ds-close-repeat twice-joining r together-ch 3 ds p-3 ds p-2 ds p-2 ds p-3 ds p-3 ds-fasten to center p of last r-ch 5 ds p-5 ds r- 5 p separated by 2 ds-close-joining center p to 3 p on cen-

Bottom 1st Row-Join thread in 2nd p on turtle back braid * ch 3 ds-p-3 ds-join to 3rd p-ch of 3 ds-p-2 ds-repeat 5 times-join to 5th p-ch of 3 ds-p-3 ds-join to 6th p-ch 5 ds-p-5 ds-clover leaf-4 ds-5 p-separated by 2 ds-ending with 4 ds-repeat twice-joining ps together as in illustration-ch 5 ds-join to p on last ch-ch 5-join to 1st p on next trutle back-ch of 3 ds-p-3 ds-join to 2nd p on braid-ch of 3 ds-p-3 ds (5 more times) join to 4th p on braid-ch 3 ds-p-3 ds-join to 5th p and 2nd p on next turtle back-repeat from * to end.

2nd Row-Join thread to 3rd p on 2nd ch on 1st row * ch 3 ds-p-3 ds (repeat 5 times)join p in next ch-ch 3 ds-p-3 ds (repeat 5 times) join p of 1st r on clover leaf-ch 3 ds-p-3 ds (repeat 5 times) join 3rd p of 2nd r on clover leaf-ch 3 ds-p-3 ds (repeat 5 times) join to 3rd p of 3rd r on clover leaf-ch 5 ds-p-3 ds (repeat 5 times) join-join p in next ch-ch 3 ds-p-3 ds (repeat 5 times) join 3rd p in next ch-ch 3 ds-p-3 ds-join to 3rd p in next ch of 5 p-repeat from * to end.

* r-4 ds-p4 ds-p-4 ds-close-ch 7 ds-p-7 ds-p-7 ds-r-4 ds-p-4 ds-p-4 ds-close-ch 9 ds-join to 2nd p of 1st

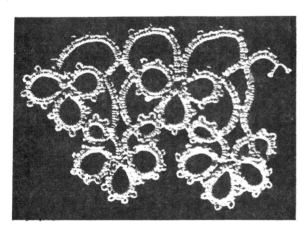

No. 10

ter r of clover leaf-ch 5 ds-make another clover leaf same as first-joining 1st p of first r to last p on small r-ch 5 ds-r of 5 p separated by 2 ds-joining 1st p to last p of last r-close 5 ds-joining to p on long ch-8 ds-join to first p on first ch made-ch 3 ds-p-2 ds p-2 ds p-3 ds p-3 ds-repeat from beginning to length required.

Turtle Back Braid with Tatting Edge

1st Row-R of dc-join to cord to braid-8 ds-close * ch of 7 ds-join in first p on straight braid-ch 7 ds-r of 5 p-separated by 4 ds-joining 4th p to first p on turtle back braid-close-make two more r same as last-joining

No. 12

ring-9 ds-join to 2nd p of 1st ring-9 ds-r-4 ds-join to p of 2nd r made-4 ds-p-4 ds-close-ch 9 ds-p-9 ds-repeat 4 more times having 72 in all-join to last p-2nd made-ch 7 ds-p-ch 7 ds * repeat from * joining 1st p of next r to p on ch between last 2 r on medallion.
Ch-4 ds-5 ps-separated by 1 ds-ending with 4 ds-with shuttle make r of 3 ps separated by 3 ds-close-ch-same as first-joining 1st p to last p of last ch-r-same as last-joining 1st p to last p of last r-repeat-ch-and r

No. 13

ps-separated by 2 ds-or same as last-skip one p on ch-fasten in next-reverse other side-ch-5 ds-r of 3 p-separated by 3 ds-ch-5 ds-and repeat from * to end. Top * r of 3 ps-separated by 3 ds-ch-8 ds-r-same as last-fastening center p on 4th p of ch-ch 8 ds-and repeat from last * to end.

Tatted Edge—* ring 7 ds-p-7 ds-close (ch 2 ds-5 p-separated by 2 ds-2 ds-ring of 7 p-join in p of 1st ring-7 ds-close) repeat 3 times more * repeat once when making 3rd scallop-join center p of 1st ch to center p

until 5 rings have been made-break-tie thread on other side of Med. and repeat from beginning to length required. Top r-2 ds-7 ps-separated by 1 ds-ending with 2 ds-close-ch-3 ds-r-same as first-joining 1st p to last p of last r-center p of r to center p of ch-ch-3 ds-make another r same as last-joining 1st p to last p of last r-ch 4 ds-9 p-separated by 1 ds-ending with 4 ds-repeat from * to end-joining together-as in illustration.

Large ring-7 ps-separated by 3 ds-close-small r-3 ps-separated by 4 ds-close-repeat small r 4 more times-joning 1st p to last p of previous r and joining to p on large r-leave thread ½ in. and repeat from beginning to length desired-joining the center p of 1st small r to

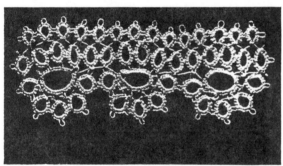

No. 14

No. 16

of last ch of 1st scallop-when making 4th scallop-join center p of 1st ch to center p of last ch of 2nd scallop-this makes scallop on both edges of lace.

center p of last scallop. Top r of 3 ps separated by 4 ds-joining center p to last p on small r-leave thread ¼ in.-make r same as last-leave thread ¼ in. and repeat across-joining on to edge as shown in illustration.

Tatting Edge—* ch of 9 ps-separated by 2 ds-r of 3 ps-separated by 4 ds-close-ch-same as 1st ch-fasten to center p on r-ch-5 ds-p-5 ds-r of 3 p-separated by 3 ds-fasten center p to 2nd p on ch-ch of 3 ps separated by 3 ds-or same as last r-joining to 3rd p on ch-ch of

Insertion

Very pretty insertion and easily made.

No. 17

One bolt novelty braid about ½ inch wide-wind shuttle without cutting thread.

1st Row—* 5 ds-p-5 ds-close-ch 7 ds-join in p on braid-7 ds-r-5 ds-join to p of 1st r-5 ds-close-repeat length desired.

2nd Row—5 r-5 ds-join in p of 1st r on 1st row-5 ds-close-ch 7 ds-join in p on braid-7 ds-r-5 ds-join in p where 1st r was joined-repeat for length of lace.
Same as Towel Edge No. 23

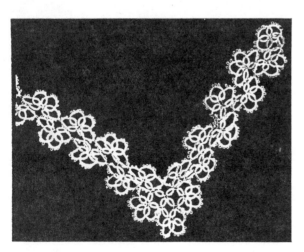

No. 15

No. 18

Same as wide edge on towel except 9 p in ring.
Blue and White Tatting on Scarf with White Thread
—Make a ring of 6 p-separated by 1 ds between each

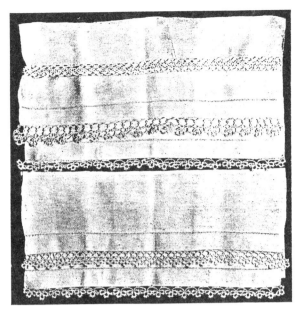

No. 20

2 ds-7 ds-r-4 ds-fasten to last p of last 2-4 ds p-4 ds-close-repeat from beginning to end of towel.

Insertion

R of 6 ds p-ch ds-close * ch 5 ds-p-2 ds p-2 ds p ending with 5 ds. Make another r same as first-joining ps together-repeat from * twice-this forms pattern and continue to end of towel.

Narrow Edge—R 5 ds-7 p separated by 1 ds-5 ds-close-make two more rs same as first-joining 1st p to last p of previous r-ch 7 ds-5 ps separated by 1 ds-5 ps-repeat from beginning across towel.

Edge on Collar

R-3 p separated by 3 ds-close-r-4 ds-p 4 ds-close-r same as 1st-joining p-r-5 ds-join to p of small r-6 p-

No. 19

p-tie on blue thread-make a ch of 7 ds-p-7 ds-p-7 ds-p-7 ds-join to 3rd p of ring-5 ds-make another ring same as first-repeat length desired-joining side p of ch. Other end of scarf—(Make a ring of white same as ring on other end-tie on blue-make a ch of 7 ds-p-7 ds) repeat joining 1st p to last p on ring just made.

Towel No. 1

R of 6 ps separated by 3 ds-close-break-r 6 ds p-fasten to first p on r-6 ds-close-repeat last r twice-joining a clover leaf-ch 6 ds-5 ps-separated by 1 ds-6 ds-r-6 ds p-fasten to next p on first r 6 ds-close-repeat last-r and ch 3 more times then repeat from beginning to length desired. Top r 6 ds-fasten to center r on first clover leaf-ch 5 ds p-2 ds p-2 ds p-ending with 5 ds-fasten to p on first r made-repeat across towel.

Towel No. 2

R 5 ds-7 p separated by 1 ds-5 ds-close-repeat r twice-joining 1st p to last p of previous r-ch 7 ds-r 4 ds-fasten to first p on last r-4 ds p and 4 ds-close-ch-7 ds-3 ps separated by 2 ds-7 ds-r-4 ds-fasten to last p of last r-4 ds p-4 ds-close-ch 7 ds-3 ps separated by

No. 21

ending with 5 ds-close-r-same as 1st-r-4 ds-join to last p on large r-4 ds-close-repeat length desired.

Handkerchief Edge

No. 100 Mercerized Cotton.

R of 5 ds-p-5 ds-ch-4 ds-p-2 ds-p-1 ds-fasten to p on first r-2 ps separated by 1 ds-ending with 3 ds-ch 3 ds-r of 6 ps separated by 1 ds fastening 1 st p to last p of last 2 ch-3 ds and repeat until rs have been made-ch 4 ds-join to p on last long ch-8 ds-p-2 ds-p-4 ds-repeat from beginning- joining p of 2 to center ps of the two rs between scallop.

69

Edging on Handkerchief

R–6 ds–p–6 ds–close with 2nd thread–ch 2 ds–5 p–separated by 2 ds ending with 2 ds–join in p of r–ch 6 ds–

No. 22

p–6 ds–r–5 ds–join to 1st p of ch over r–5 ds–join–ch 2 ds–3 p separated by 2 ds–ending with 2 ds–r same as last–joining next p of ch over r–repeat twice–making 4 r on

No. 24

larger rs of 7 ps separated by 2 ds in each–break–fasten thread in first large r–ch 4 ps–separated by 3 ds–r of 3 ps–separted by 3 ds–close–ch same as last–r same as last–joining first p to last p of previous r–repeat–ch–r–3 ds–p–3 ds–join to p on large r–3 ds–p–3 ds–close–ch same as last–joining to center p of next large r–repeat–ch once more–break–make other wing in same manner. Lower wing—R of 7 p–separated by 2 ds–close–ch of 15 p–separated by 2 ds–make p all around same as 1st r on first r–repeat on other side–break.

No. 23

ch–ch 6 ds p–6 ds–join where 1st r was started–ch 2 ds–5 p separated by 2 ds–ending with 2 ds allowing ch to go under 1st r made–ch 6 ds–r of 5 ds–p–5 ds–close 6 ds and repeat pattern.

Tatted Butterfly

Very effective in table runner, piano scarf, etc.

Ch–8 ds–p–8 ds–made small ring–4 ds–1 long p–2 ds–1 long p–4 ds–close–ch of 4 p–separated by 2 ds–join to p on first ch–4 p–separated by 2 ds–join to end of ch–repeat on other side of ch–break–this forms body. R of 9 ps–separated by 2 ds–close–ch of 22 ps–separated by 2 ds–r of 4 ds–p–4 ds–p–4 ds–p–ending with 4 ds–leave ⅛ inch thread and repeat 9 times–joining rings together and joining to ch–as shown in illustration–then make 6

Tatted Doily

R of 3 ds–p–3 ds–p–3 ds–p–3 ds–close–leave ⅛ inch thread–make another r same as 1st–joining side p–r–3 ds–join to last p of small r–2 ds–7 p–separated by 2 ds–3 ds–close–repeat from beginning 12 times more–cut and tie thread–r of 4 ds–p–4 ds–p–4 ds–p–4 ds–close–ch 5 ds–p–5 ds–r–join to 1st p to last–p of 1st r–ch 4 ds–p–3 ds–

No. 25

r–join to side p of last r–ch 3 ds–r–2 ds–7 p separated by 2 ds–3 ds–close ch–3 ds–r like 1st–join 1st p of 2 to last p of large r–ch 3 ds–join to p of ch between 2nd and 3rd r–ch 4 ds another r like 1st joining side p–ch 5 ds–join to p of ch between 1st and 2nd r–ch 5 ds–r like 1st joining side p–ch 4 ds–p–4 ds–join to p of 1st small r on 1st round–4 ds–join to p of 2nd small r of 1st round–ch 4 ds–p–4 ds–repeat around–joining center p of 1st ring of 2nd scallop to center p of last r of 1st scallop.

Directions for Yoke or Centerpiece on Cover

R of 3 ps separated by 4 ds–close–repeat twice–joining 1st p to last p of previous r–12 ds p–6 ds–make 3 more rs same as first three–6 ds–joining to p on ch–12 ds p–6 ds–r of 9 long p separated by 2 ds–close–ch 6 ds–make r same as last–joining first p to last p of last r–6 ds–repeat r once more–ch 6 ds–join to p on ch–ch 12 ds p–6 ds–make 3 more rs same as first 3 rings–ch 6–join to p on ch–6 ds–join to 3 first r made–break–r of 9 long p–separated by 2 ds–joining 3rd p to p on last r made–ch 6–ch 6 ds–r of 9 ps–separated by 2 ds–close * ch 6 ds p–6 ds p–3 ds p–3 ds p–6 ds p–6 ds–join to center p on last r–ch 6 ds–r same as last–joining center p

ing to next p on ch–ch 6 ds–make another leaf–join to point–make two more leaves on other side–break–repeat in each point in same manner–Med in front point r of 8 p separated by 3 ds–close–break–fasten thread in p–ch 6 ds p–6 ds p–6 ds p–6 ds–fasten to next p on–repeat all around–break next round–fasten thread in first p–ch 8 ds–fasten in center p–ch 8–fasten in next two ps–repeat around–break–top r of 3 ps separated by 4 ds–joining center p in ch on yoke * ch 8 ds–3 ps separated by 2 ds–8 ds–r same as first–fasten to r on yoke–repeat from * all around as shown in illustration and joining Med. in point. Next row same as outside edge around yoke–joining ps on ch together.

No. 26

to center r on the 1st piece made–ch 6 ds–r same as last–close–ch–6 ds–join to p on ch–6 ds–3 ps separated by one ds–6 ds p–6 ds–join to center p on last r made–ch 6 ds–r–ch 6 ds r–repeat from * 2 more times except front point–repeat 3 times–ch 6–fasten to p on last ch–ch–6 ds p–2 ds p–2 ds p–ch–6 ds p–6 ds–fasten to center p on last r–ch–6 ds–r ch 6 ds–r–ch 6 ds–fasten to p on ch–6 ds–fasten to next p on same ch–ch 2 ds p–2 ds p–6 ds p–6 ds–fasten to center p on last 2–this forms point. Reverse for other side–joining ps as shown in illustration leaf for inside of points–ch 12–long ps–separated by one ds–join to p on ch–ch 12 long ps–fasten where work was begun–ch 12 ds–make another leaf same as first–join–

This also makes a very attractive centerpiece, omitting point in front.

Luncheon Set, No. 27
No. 20 Mercerized Cotton

R of 6 p–separated by 2 ds–close–break * r–5 ds p–3 ds p–fasten to any p on first r–3 ds p ending with 5 ds–close–ch 5 ds–3 p separated by 2 ds–5 ds–repeat from * 5 more times–break–make each Med. separately–joining them together as shown in illustration.

Collar, No. 28

Ch–14 ds–with 1 long p between each ds * r–2 ds–p–2 ds–fasten to long p–2 ds p–2 ds–leave thread ¼ in.–

r–3 ds–p–4 p–separated by 2 ds–ending with 3 ds–leave thread ¼ in.–repeat from * all around–fasten off–r of 3 ds–fasten to center of p of any r–4 p–separated by 2 ds–ending with 3 ds–repeat twice–fastening p to last p of previous r–break–this forms point of Med.–make each Med. separately–joining two rings together–edge around r 3 ds–fasten to center p on r–3 ds–close–ch–4 ds–p–4 ds–repeat all around.

Pointed Edge Lace, No. 29

(Ring of 8 long p–separated by 2 ds–cut and tie thread–ring of 3 ds–p–3 ds–join to p of center ring–3 ds–p–3 ds–close–ch–5 ds–5 p–separated by 3 ds–5 ds) repeat 7 times more–join–cut thread–ring of 5 ds–p–3 ds–p–

Top edge of point lace—Ring of 4 ds–p–4 ds–join in 4th p of 1st ch of top–4 ds–p–4 ds–close–leave a short length of thread each time (small ring of 3 ds–p–3 ds–ring–4 ds–join to last p of large ring–4 ds–join to 2nd p of next ch on medallion–4 ds–p–4 ds–close–ring–3 ds–close–large ring–join center p to 4th p on same ch–repeat twice more–small ring–large ring–join to 2nd p of next ch on medallion–small ring–join p to p of last small ring–large ring–to go between medallions–small ring–large ring–join to 4th p on 1st ch of next medallion–repeat pattern the length of lace–joining 2 small rings together each time and joining large rings by side p each time. Upper row—Same as lower row–only joining 2 small rings to the 2 small rings in lower row and leaving center p of large rings to sew on lace by.

No. 27

3 ds–p–3 ds–join to center p of ch on ring–3 ds–p–5 ds–close–another ring like 1st–joining 2nd p to center p of next ch on wheel–another ring–cut and tie thread–ring of 3 ds–p–3 ds–join in p next to where 1st of 3 rings were joined to wheel–3 ds–p–3 ds–close–ch of 5 ds–5 p–separated by 2 ds–5 ds–ring–join center p to 1st p of 1st of 3 rings–ch–ring–join to 2nd p of next ring–ch–ring–join center p to 4th p of same ring–ch–ring–join to 1st p of next ring–ch–ring–join to next p to where 2nd of 3 rings were joined–ch–ring–join in center p of next ch on wheel (ch–ring–join to 2nd p of next ch on wheel–ring–join to 4th p of same ch) repeat 3 times more–ch–join to center p of next ch on wheel–ch–join to 1st ring on outside round–join sides of medallions together by center p of 2 ch–leaving 7 ch around points and 5 ch over top.

Pointed Yoke, No. 30

Wind shuttle without cutting thread–5 p separated by 2 ds–close * ch 2 p–repeat last 4 more times–ending with 2 ds–r–2 ds–p–2 ds–join to 4th p of 1st ring–finish r same as first–repeat from * 5 more times–this finishes one wheel. Ch 2 p–repeat last 6 more times–ending with 2 ds–r–5 p–separated by 2 ds–close ch same as last of 7 p–repeat from beginning joining wheels together same as shown in illustration. Top R—3 p separated by 4 ds–turn–work–leave a short piece of thread and make another r–continue making r–turning after each and joining to previous one of that row and joining every other r to 3rd p on ch.

No. 28

No. 29

73

No. 70 Cotton.

Make a ring of 7 long p-separated by 7 ds-cut and tie thread-make a ring of 3 ds-p-3 ds-join to p of center ring-3 ds-p-3 ds-tie on other thread and make ch of 4 ds-p (2 ds-p) repeat three times making 5 p in all

length of thread between each ring-makea small ring of 5 ds-p-5 ds-close-4 ds-join to side p of 1st ring-4 ds-join to 3 p on ch of same side wheel-4 ds-p-4 ds-close-joining in p of 1st small ring-large ring joining side p to large ring last made and center p to 2nd p of ch on corner wheel-make another large ring-join side p to ring last made and center p to 4th p of corner wheel-make another large ring- joining to p of last ring

No. 30

4 ds * repeat from * to * six times and cut thread and join outside row of wheel-make same as inside row except joining two rings to p of every other ch-and one ring to every other ch-make 20 wheels joining to form square yoke. Inside rows of yoke—1st row for corner-make a ring of 4 ds-p-4 ds-join to first p of ch-on side wheel next to corner wheel-4 ds-p-4 ds-close-leave short

made and center p to center p of ch on wheel next to corner-another small ring joining to p of 1st small ring made.

Camisole. No. 32

No. 20 Mercerized Cotton

Work with one thread throughout large r-3 ps separated by 4 ds-close-leave thread ¼ inch-make small r-4 ds-p-4 ds-close-leave thread ¼ inch-make large r same as 1st-joining 1st p to last p of large r-leave ¼ inch thread-make small r-same as last-joining ps together-leave thread ¼ inch-repeat from beginning for length required-make another strip same as 1st-joining small rs together. Top—Large r same as 1st-joining center p to center p on strip-leave thread ¼ inch-make small r-same as 1st-close-leave thread ¼ inch-make large r-joining 1st p to last p of last r and center p to center p on strip-leave thread ¼ inch and make large r of 4 ds-fasten to p on small r-7 ps-separated by 1 ds-ending with 4 ds-close-leave thread ¼ inch-large r-same as before-leave thread ¼ inch-make small r-joining to last p on large r and repeat across straps-across shoulder same as 1st strip.

Tatted Bag, No. 33

No. 10 Mercerized Cotton.

R of 3 p-separated by 4 ds-close-make 3 more rings same as first-break-repeat from beginning 8 more times joining center p together as shown in illustration-r of 3 ps separated by 4 ds-close-ch 3 ps separated by 4 ds-r of 3 ps separated by 4 ds-joining center p to center p on medallion-repeat on both sides of medallion-break-r of 3 p separated by 4 ds-ch 6 ds-make another r joining center p to center p on ch of previous row-ch 6 ds and

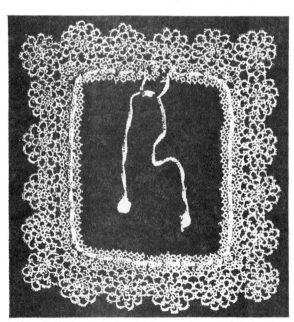

No. 31

No. 32

repeat to end of row—break—center row of medallion—
r of 5 ps separated by 2 ds—close—ch 4 ds—5 ps separated
by 2 ds—ending with 4 ds—repeat 6 more times joining

same as first—joining center p to 1st p on bag—ch 4 ds—
fasten to 4 ds of last ch—ch 4 ds and repeat from *
around.

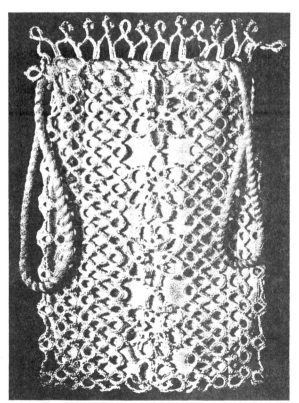

No. 33

together as shown in illustration—make 8 more medallions in same manner and reverse other side of bag.
Top—R of 3 ps separated by 5 ds—close—ch 8 ds * r of
3 ps separated by 4 ds—close—ch 8 ds—make another r

Dresser Scarf, No. 34

R of 7—ds—11 p separated by 2 ds—7 ds—close—repeat
twice with 2nd thread—ch 7—dc—4 p separated by 2 ds—

75

7 ds–r of 3 ds–p–3 ds–p–3 ds–close–ch of ds–5 p–separated by 2 ds–4 small r in each large r–make last ch like 1st–joining where 1st ch started and joining last p of last ch to 1st p of 1st ch–join medallions between 2nd and 3rd r on side–make as many medallions as desired for length of scarf.

fasten to last p of previous r–2 p–separated by 2 ds–fasten to center p on medallion–finish r with 3 p–separated by 1 ds–ending with 3 ds–close–make another r–same as first–ch–2 ds–11 ps–separated by 1 ds–ending with 2 ds–repeat from last * all around–next 4 rounds same as 1st round–last round same as 2nd round.

No. 34

Upper edge—R of 4 ds–p–4 ds–join to center p of 1st short ch–4 ds–p–4 ds–close–ch 4 ds–5 p separated by 2 ds ending with 4 ds–r joining 2nd p to first p and long ch–ch like 1st–r joining to last p of next long ch–ring–join in center of next short ch–repeat in every medallion to end.

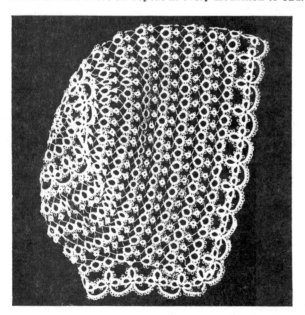

No. 35

No. 36

Small Edge—R of 5 ds–5 p separated by 2 ds ending with 5 ds–close–ch 4 ds–3 p separated by 3 ds–ending with 4 ds–repeat–joining 1st p to last p of last r.

Baby Cap, No. 35

R 3 ds–7 ds–separated by 1 ds–ending with 3 ds–close–repeat 3 more times–break * r–2 ds–p–2 ds–fasten to 3rd p–on large r–2 ds–p–2 ds–close–leave thread ¼ in.–r of 3 ds–7 p–separated by 1 ds–ending with 3 ds–close–leave thread ¼ in.–repeat from * all around–break–r–3 ds–5 p–separated by 1 ds–3 ds–close–r–3 ds–

Baby Dress, No. 36

Wind shuttle–don't cut thread.

R–3 p separated by 3 ds–close–r–7 ch–9 ds * r–3 * separated by 3 ds–ch 9 ds–r–joining 1st p to last p of 1st ring–repeat from * to length required.

Edge for Neck and Sleeves—R–5 p separated by 2 ds–close–leave thread ¼ inch and proceed the length joining each r to previous l by 1st p.

76

15 TATTED YOKES & CAMISOLES

FINISHED ON SATIN

All yokes shown in this book are as close to size 36 as the Motifs will permit. Half the Yoke as shown is 18 inches. With this as a guide you will be able to judge your work.

SEE INSTRUCTIONS on Page 91

See abbreviations on Page 78

SHOWN OVER HALF ACTUAL SIZE

BOOK 9 BY Anna Valeire

TATTED YOKE No. 2

Made in No. 30 Crochet Cotton. Requires 3 Balls.

Square Medallion. c-r, 2d (long p, 2d) 8 times. Tie and cut threads. On two shuttles, continuous thread between, L-r, 5d, j to p of c-r, 2d p, 2d, j to next p of c-r, 5d, p, (3d, p) 4 times, close, turn. *Ch 2d, (p, 2d) 3 times, turn, r 5d, j to p of large r, 5d close, turn. Repeat from * 4 more times. NOTE—see corner c-leaf below. Then repeat from beginning 3 times, fasten at base of first large ring, tie and cut.

NOTE—Corner c-leaf can be worked separately and sewed, or as you reach the third ch of 3b—thus 2d, p, turn, s-r, 2d, j to p just made (2d, p) 4 times 2d, close. Three such rings for clover, turn, ch 1d, 2d, p, 2d and resume medallion mit. As medallions are completing join 2 r of c-leaf on 2 adjoining picots.

Top Edge. C-leaf, each, r 3d-(p, 3d) 5 times, close, 3 rings, turn, ch 5d, p, 5d-(p, 2d) 3 times, turn. Larger r, 3d- (p, 1f) 5 times, j to p of 2 c-leaf, (1d, p) 5 times, 3d close, then reverse motif to center of next c-leaf. Joining by these third picots to corner clovers, and j ch as working up to center of clover, of edge.

All yokes shown in this book are as close to size 36 as the Motifs will permit. Half the Yoke as shown is 18 inches. With this as a guide you will be able to judge your work.

ABBREVIATIONS

sh—shuttles.	betw—between
sq—square.	ch—chain.
s-r—small ring	c-r—center ring.
( )—means repeat all that is	d—doubles.
shown in ( ) as many times	j—join.
as told.	L-r—large ring.
*—star is a sign of start of	med—medallion
longer motif.	p—picot.
	r—ring.

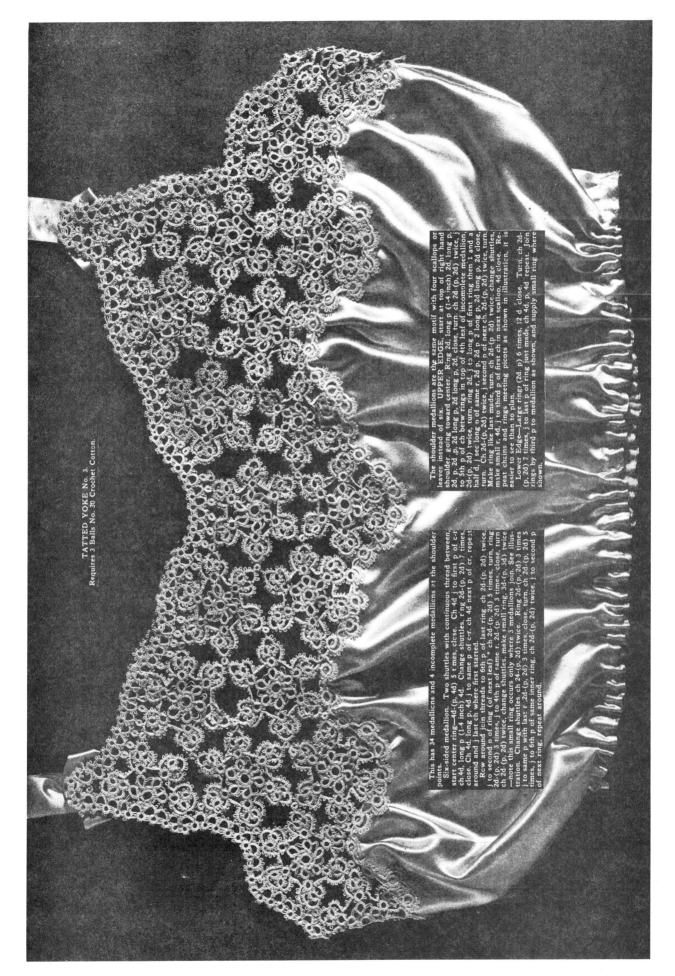

TATTED YOKE No. 3.
Requires 3 Balls No. 30 Crochet Cotton.

This has 34 medallions and 4 incomplete medallions at the shoulder points.

Six-sided medallion. Two shuttles with continuous thread between, start center ring—4d-(p, 4d) 5 times, close. Ch 4d j to first p of c-r, ch 4d, long p (1-4 inch) 4d. Change shuttles, r ng 2d-(p, 2d) 7 times, close. Ch 4d, long p, 4d j to same p of c-r, ch 4d next p of c-r, repeat around and j last ch where first started.

Row around join threads to 6th p of last ring, ch 2d-(p, 2d) twice, j to second p of ring (of next leaf)* ch 2d-(p, 2d) 5 times, turn, ring 2d-(p, 2d) 3 times, j to 4th p of same r, 2d-(p, 2d) 3 times, close, turn ch 2d-(p, 2d) twice, change shuttles, make small ring, 3d-(p, 3d) twice —note this small ring occurs only where 3 medallions join. See illustration. Change shuttles, ch 24-(p, 2d) twice, Ring 2d-(p, 2d) 3 times j to same p with last r 2d-(p, 2d) 3 times, close, turn, ch 2d-(p, 2d) 5 times, j to 6th p of same inner ring, ch 2d-(p, 2d) twice, j to second p of next ring, repeat around.

The shoulder medallions are the same motif with four scallops or leaves instead of six. UPPER EDGE, start at top of right hand shoulder, going toward center. Ring 2d, long p (1-4 inch) 2d, long p, 2d, p, 2d long p, 2d long p, 2d, close, turn, ch 2d-(p, 2d) twice, j to 5th p of ch betw rings in top of 4th leaf of incomplete medallion, 2d-(p, 2d) twice, turn, ring 2d, j to long p of first ring then l and a half d, j sec long p of same r, 2d p, 2d p 2 long p, 2d long p, 2d close, turn. Ch 2d-(p, 2d) twice, j second p of next ch 2d-(p, 2d) twice, turn. Make ring like last made, turn, ch 2d-(p, 2d) twice, change shuttles, make small r, 4d, j to third p of first ch in next scallop, 4d close. Repeat chains and rings meeting picots as shown in illustration, it is easier to see than to plan.

Lower Edge—Large ring, (2d, p) 6 times, 12 d, close. Turn, ch 2d-(p, 2d) 7 times, j to last p of ring just made, ch 4d, p, 4d repeat. Join rings by third p to medallion as shown, and supply small ring where shown.

79

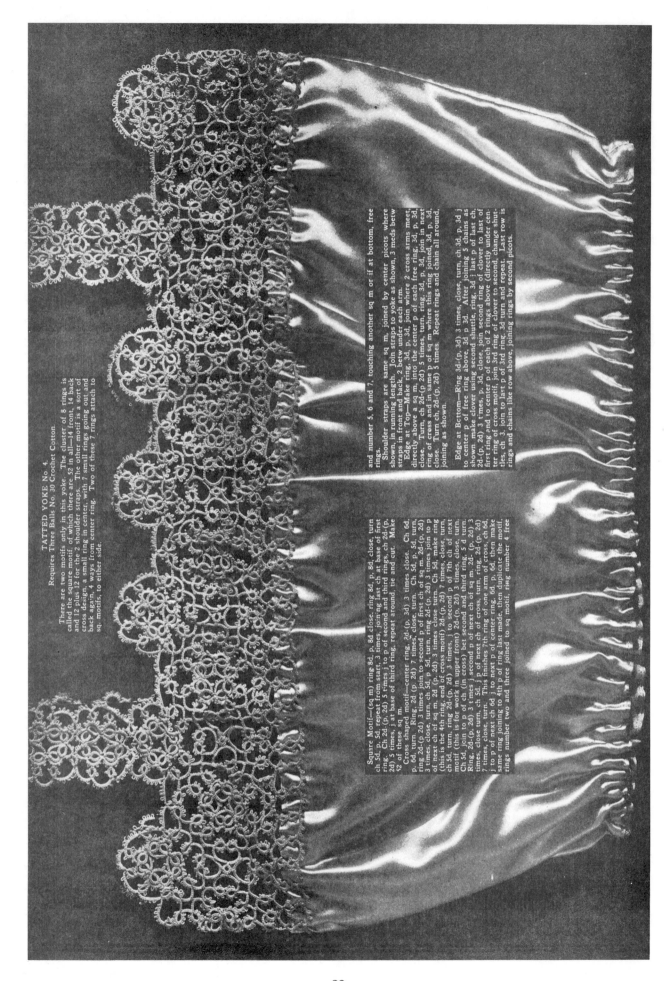

TATTED YOKE No. 4.
Requires Three Balls No. 30 Crochet Cotton.

There are two motifs only in this yoke. The cluster of 8 rings is called the square motif of which there are 52 in all—14 front, 14 back and 12 plus 12 for the 2 shoulder straps. The other motif is a sort of cross design, a small ring in center, with 7 small rings going out and back again, 4 ways from center ring. Two of these 7 rings attach to sq. motifs, to either side.

Square Motif.—(sq. m) ring 8d, p, 8d close, ring 8d, p, 8d, close, turn ch 5d, p, 5d, repeat from start, 3 times, joining last ch at base of first ring. Ch 2d, (p, 2d) 5 times to p of second and third rings, ch 2d-(p, 2d) 5 times, j at base of third ring, repeat around, tie and cut. Make 52 of these sq. m.

Cross shaped motif—center ring, 2d-(p, 3d) 3 times close, Ch 6d, p, 6d turn. Ring, 2d-(p, 2d) 7 times, close, turn. Ch 5d, 5d, turn, ring 2d-(p, 2d) 3 times join to second p of first ch of sq m, 2d-(p, 2d) 3 times, close, turn, 5d, p, 5d, turn, ring 2d-(p, 2d) 3 times join to p of next ch of sq m, 2d (p, 2d) 3 times close turn, Ch 5d, make ring (this is the 4th ring, end of cross motif) 2d-(p, 2d) 7 times, close, turn, ch 5d, turn, ring 2d-(p, 2d) 3 times, j to second p of 7th ch of next motif (this is for work in upper front) 2d-(p, 2d) 3 times, close, turn, Ch 5d, join to p of ch (in cross) bet second and third ring, 5 d turn. Ring, 2d-(p, 2d) 3 t'mes ; second p of next ch of sq m. 2d-(p, 2d) 3 times, close turn, ch 5d, j p of next ch of cross, turn, ring, 2d-(p, 2d) 7 times, close, turn. This finishes 7th ring of one arm of cross, ch 6d, j to p of next ch 6d j to next p of center ring, 6d, p, 6d, then make same ring joining to 4th p of ring last made, then duplicate the motif, rings number two and three joined to sq motif ring number 4 free

and number 5, 6 and 7, touching another sq m or if at bottom, free rings.

Shoulder straps are same sq. m, joined by center picots where shown, in running length. Join straps to yoke as shown, 3 meds betw straps in front and back, 2 betw under each arm.

Edge at Top—Make ring, 3d, p, 3d, join where 2 cross arms meet, directly above a sq m. into the center p of each free ring, 3d, p, 3d, close. Turn, ch 2d-(p 2d) 5 times, turn, ring, 3d, p, 3d, join in next ring of cross and in same p of sq m where this ring joined, 3d, p 3d, close. Turn ch, 2d-(p, 2d) 5 times Repeat rings and chain all around, joining as shown.

Edge at Bottom—Ring 3d-(p, 3d) 3 times, close, turn, ch 3d, p, 3d j to center p of free ring above, 3d p 3d. After joining 5 chains as shown make clover using second shuttle, ring, 3d ; last p of last ch, 2d-(p, 2d) 3 t'mes, p, 3d, close, join second ring of clover to last of first ring and to center p of each of 2 rings above (directly under center ring of cross motif, join 3rd ring of clover to second, change shuttles, ch 3, join to last p of 3rd ring, 3d turn and repeat. Last row is rings and chains like row above, joining rings by second picots.

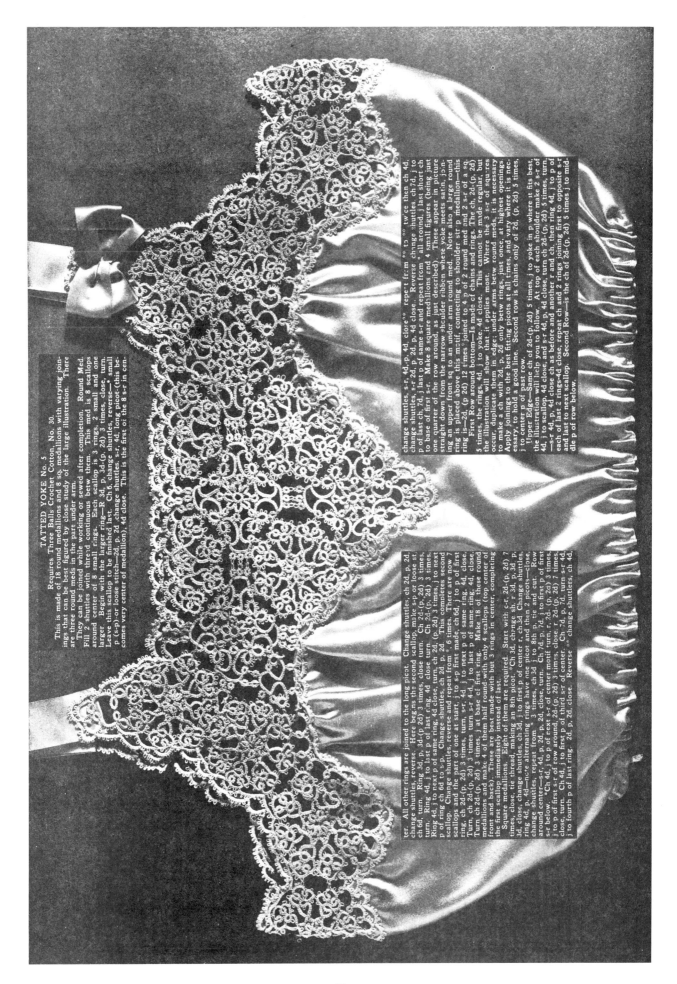

TATTED YOKE No. 5

This is made of 18 round medallions and 8 sq. medallions with varying joinings that can be best figured by close study of the large illustration. There are three round meds in the part under arm.

Requires Three Balls Crochet Cotton, No. 30.

They can be joined while working or sewed after completion. **Round Med.** Fill 2 shuttles with thread continuous betw them. This med is 8 scallops around center of 8 small rings. Each scallop is 3 rings, 2 small and one larger. Begin with the larger ring—R 3d, p 3d-(p, 2d) 3 times, close, turn. Leave this scallop to be finished last. Ch 6, change shuttles, reverse—* small p (s-p) or loose stitch—2d, p 2d ,change shuttles, s-r, 4d. long picot (this becomes very center of medallion), 4d close. This is the first oi the 8 s-r in cen-

ter. All other rings are joined to the long picot. Change shuttles, ch 2d, 2d, change shuttles, reverse. Here begins the second scallop, make s-p or loose st, ch 6d, turn. Ring 3d, p, 3d-(p 2d) 3 times, close. Change sh-r 3d, p, 3d, p, turn. Ring 4d, j to last p of last ring. 4d close, turn. Ch 2d-(p, 2d) 3 times, change shuttles. Ring 4d, j to next p of same ring, 4d close, turn, ch 2d, (p, 2d) 3 times, j to next p of ring ch 6d to s-p. Change shuttles, reverse and repeat from * 6 times. This completes second scallop and the part of one at start, j to s-p first made, ch 6d, j to p of first ring, ch 2d-(p, 2d) 3 times, turn, s-r, 4d, j to next p of same ring, 4d close. Turn, ch 2d-(p, 2d) 3 times, j at base of first ring. Make 18 of these round medallions and make 4 of them half round-with only 4 scallops (top center of front and back). These are best made with but 3 rings in center, completing the first scallop immediately instead of last.

Square Medallions. Eight of them are required. Start with c-r, 2d-(p, 2d) 7 times, close, tie thread, making an 8th picot. Ch 3d, change sh-r 3d, p, 3d, p, 3d, close, change shuttles, ch 3d, j to first p of center r, ch 3d, Change shuttles, ring 4d, p, 4d,—more alternating rings have one picot and then 2 picots—close, change shuttles, repeat from ° 3 times, ch 3d, turn, r, 2d, close, turn. Ch 7d, p, 7d, j to first p of first s-r below. Ch 4d, j to p of next s-r of center motif turn, r, 2d- (p, 2d) 3 times, j top of first s-r of row around, 2d-(p, 2d) 3 times, close, r, 2d-(p, 2d) 7 times, close, turn. Ch 7d, p, 7d, turn s-r, 4d, close, turn. Ch 4d, j to first p of third s-r of center. Reverse,° change shuttles, ch 4d,

change shuttles, s-r, 4d.-p, 4d close°° repe t fr.m ** t) °° tw c then ch 4d. change shuttles, s-r 2d. p 2d.p, 4d close. Reverse chnge shuttles, ch 7d, j to p of last ch, 7d, j last p of same s-r and repeat from * all around, j last short ch to base of first s-r. Make 8 square medallions and 4 small figures (being just one quarter of the row around, as just described). These appear in picture straight down from the narrow shoulder ribbon where yoke meets satin, joining an upper front sq to an under arm round med. .Note also a large round ring is placed above this motif, connecting to shoulder str p medallion—this ring is—2d, (p 2d) 12 times joined to 4 p of 2 round med and 2 s-r of a sq.

First Row around bottom—is made of chains and rings. The ch, 2d-(p, 2d) 5 times, the rings, 4d, j to yoke, 4d close. This cannot be made regular, but the illustration will show that it applies most. Where the 3 s-r of squ res occur, duplicate them in edge; under arms betw round meds, it is necessary to make a ch with 2d, p, 2d only betw rings, just once, at highest openings. Apply joinings to the best fitting picots at all times, and vary where it is necessary, to hold a good line. Second row is chains only of 2d, (p, 2d) 5 times, j to center p of past row.

Upper Edge—Same ch of 2d-(p, 2d) 5 times, j to yoke in p where it fits best, the illustration will help you to follow. At top of each shoulder make 2 s-r of 4d, j to scallop, 4d close, and s-r 4d, p, 4d close, turn ch 2d-(p, 2d) 5 times, turn, —s-r 4d, p, 4d close ch as before and another r and ch, then ring 4d, j to p of each of last 2 rings-4d close, repeat ch and 2 rings joining first to opposite s-r and last to next scallop. Second Row—is the ch of 2d-(p, 2d) 5 times j to middle p of row below.

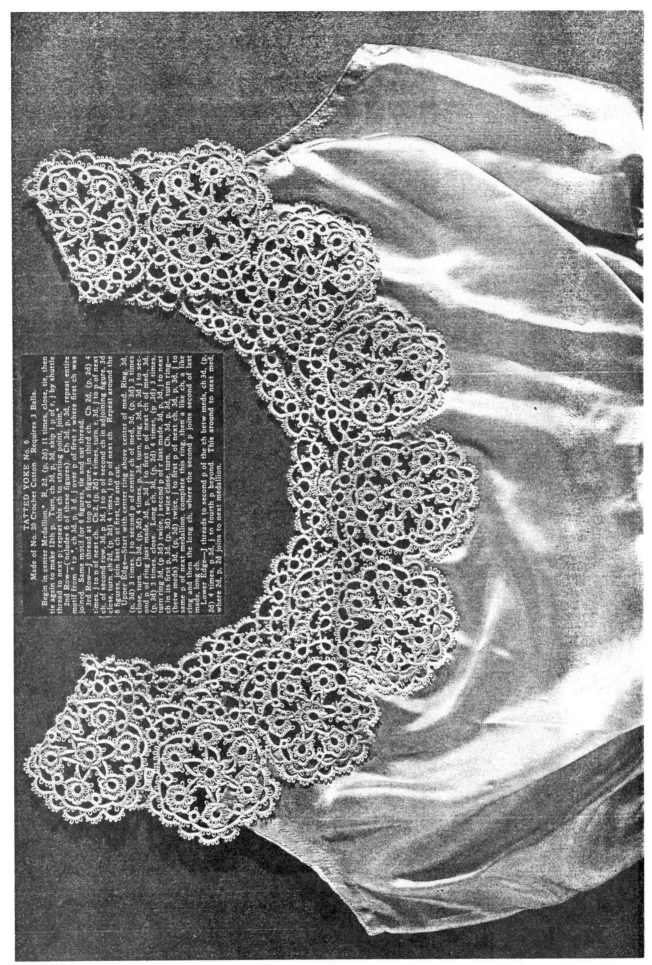

TATTED YOKE No. 6

Made of No. 30 Crochet Cotton. Requires 3 Balls.

Begin in center Medallion*. R. 2 d, (p, 2 d) 11 times, close, tie, then tie again to make 12th p. Turn. Ch 3 d, p, 3 d, skip 1 p, of r, j by shuttle thread to next p; repeat this ch to starting point, join.*

2nd Row—(includes 6 of these figures). Ch 3 d, p, 3 d, repeat entire motif from * to *, ch 3 d, p, 3 d, j over p of first r where first ch was joined. Same motif for 6 figures, tie and cut thread.

3rd Row—J thread at top of a figure, in third ch. Ch 2 d, (p, 2 d) 4 times, j to p of next ch. Ch 2, (p, 2 d) 4 times, turn, r 3 d, j to p of next ch. of second row, 3 d, p 3 d, j to p of second ch in adjoining figure, 3 d close, turn, ch 2 d, (p, 2 d) 4 times, j to p of next ch. Repeat around the 6 figures, join last ch at first, tie and cut.

Upper Edge—Start with center ring above, center of med. Ring, 3 d, (p, 3 d) 3 times, j to second p of center ch of med, 3 d, (p, 3 d) 3 times close, turn. Ch 3 d, (p, 2 d) 4 times, p, 3 d, turn, ring, 3 d, p, 3 d j to second p of ring just made, 3 d, p, 3 d j to first p of next ch of med, 3 d, (p, 3 d) 3 times, close. Long ch, 3 d, (p, 2 d) 4 times, (p, 3 d) 3 times, turn ring 3 d, (p 3 d) twice, j second p of last made, 3 d, p, 3 d, j to next ch in its first p, 3 d, (p, 3 d) twice close, turn. Ch, 3 d, p, 3 d, turn ring— (betw meds) 3 d, (p, 3 d) twice, j to first p of next ch, 3 d, p, 3 d, j to same p of next medallion, complete this ring, then a like ch, a like ring and then the long ch, where the second p joins second of last made, long ch.

Lower Edge—J threads to second p of the ch betw meds, ch 3 d, (p, 2 d) 4 times, p, 3 d, j to fourth p beyond. This around to next med, where 2 d, p, 2 d joins to next medallion.

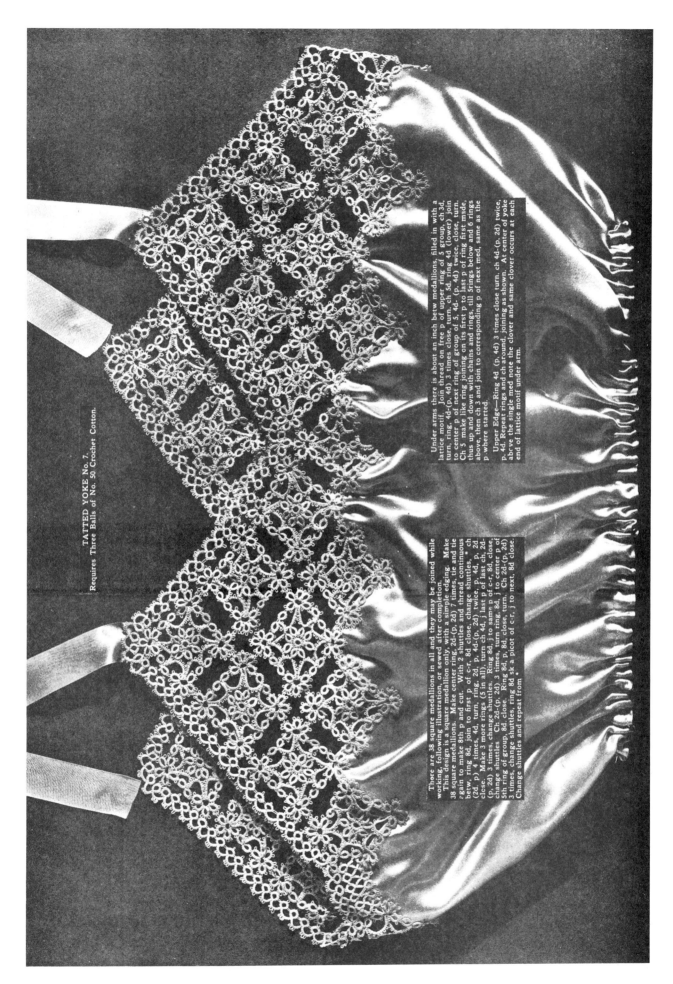

TATTED YOKE No. 7.
Requires Three Balls of No. 50 Crochet Cotton.

There are 38 square medallions in all and they may be joined while working, following illustration, or sewed after completion.

This design is a square medallion only, with a simple edging. Make 38 square medallions. Make center ring, 2d-(p, 2d) 7 times, tie and tie again to make 8th p and cut. With 2 shuttles and thread continuous betw. ring 8d, join to first p, of c-r 8d close, change shuttles, * ch (2d, p,) 4 times, 4d, turn, ring, 2d, p, 4d-(p, 2d) twice, p, 4d, p, 2d close. Make 3 more rings (5 in all), turn ch 4d, j last p of last ch, 2d-(p, 2d) 3 times, change shuttles. Ring 8d, j to same p of c-r, 8d, close, change shuttles. Ch 2d-(p, 2d) 3 times, turn ring, 8d, j to center p of 5th ring of group, 8d, close. Ring 8d, p, 8d, close, turn. Ch 2d-(p, 2d) 3 times, change shuttles, ring 8d k a picot of c-r, j ro next, 8d close. Change shuttles and repeat from *

Under arms there is about an inch betw. medallions, filled in with a lattice motif. Join thread on free p of upper ring of 5 group, ch 3d, turn, ring, 4d-(p, 4d) 3 times close, turn, ch 5d, ring 4d (lower) join to center p of next ring of group of 5, 4d-, (p, 4d) twice, close, turn. Ch 5 make like ring joining on its first p to last p of ring first made, thus up and down with chains and rings, till 5rings below and 6 rings above, then ch 3 and join to corresponding p of next med, same as the p where started.

Upper Edge—Ring 4d (p, 4d) 3 times close turn, ch 4d-(p, 2d) twice, p, 4d. Repeat rings and ch around, joining as shown. At center of yoke abrve the single med note the clover and same clover occurs at each end of lattice motif under arm.

83

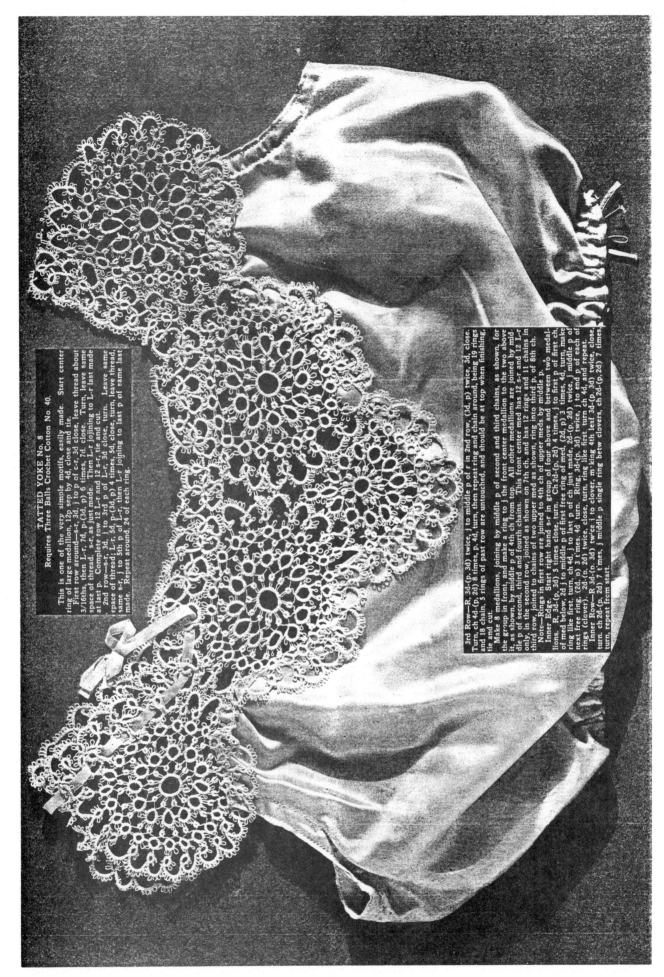

TATTED YOKE No. 8
Requires Three Balls Crochet Cotton No. 40.

This is one of the very simple motifs, easily made. Start center ring of large medallion, 12p sep by 4d, close and tie.

First row around—s-r, 3d, j to p of c-r, 3d close, leave thread about 3/16ths, then L-r, 7d, p-(3d, p) 6 times, 7d close. Turn, leave same space of thread, s-r, as just made. Then L-r joining to L-r last made at last p. Complete row 12 L-r and 12 s-r, tie and cut.

2nd row—s-r, 3d, j to 3rd p of L-r, 3d close, turn. Leave same space of thread; L-r, 5d, j to p-(3d, p) 4 times, 5d close, turn. Leave thread, same s-r, j to 5th p of L-r, then L-r joining to last p of same last made. Repeat around 24 of each ring.

3rd Row—R, 3d-(p, 3d) twice, j to middle p of r in 2nd row, (3d, p) twice, 3d, close. Turn, ch 4d-(p, 2d) 8 times, 4d, turn, then repeating ring and chain around, being 19 rings and 18 chain, 5 rings of past row are untouched, and should be at top when finishing, tie and cut.

Make 8 medallions, joining by middle p of second and third chains, as shown, for the group in front, and make a ring to j the front center medallion to the two above it, as shown, by middle p of 4th ch from top. All other medallions are joined by middle p of second, third and fourth chains. This front center med has 12 s-r and 12 L-r only, in the second row, joined as shown on 7th ch, and has 12 rings and 11 chains in third row, joined to chains of two upper med as shown, ring into third p. of 8th ch.

Note—Rings in first row are joined to 4th ch of upper meds by middle p.

Inner Edge. Start right hand s-r in group of four above and between two medallions. R, 3d-(p, 3d) 5 times close, turn. Ch 2d-(p, 2d) 4 times, j to first p of first ch. of med below, 2d j to middle p of first free ring of med. (2d, p.) 3 times, 4d, turn, make ring like first, turn. ch 4d, j to last p of ch just made, 2d-(p, 2d) twice, j middle p of next free ring, (2d, p.) 3 times, 4d turn. Ring, 3d-(p, 3d) twice, j to end p of each of rings (clover). 2d-(n, 2d) twice, close, turn. Ring like first turn ch 4d, and repeat.

Inner Row—R 3d-(n, 3d) twice, j to clover, close, turn. Ring like first 3d-(p, 3d) twice, close, turn. ch 2d-(p, 2d) 7 t'mes, j middle p single ring betw clovers, ch 2d-(p, 2d) 7 times, turn, repeat from start.

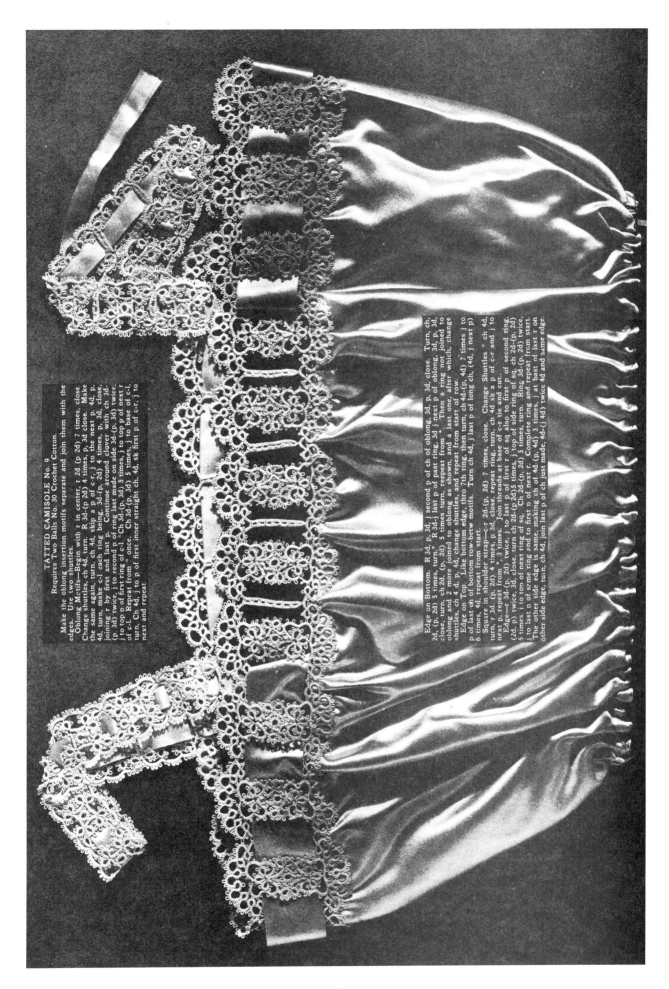

TATTED CAMISOLE No. 9
Requires Two Balls No. 30 Crochet Cotton.
Make the oblong insertion motifs separate and join them with the edges. Use two shuttles.

Oblong Motifs—Begin with r in center, r 2d (p 2d) 7 times, close. Change shuttles, ch 4d, turn.* R 3d-(p 2d) 4 times, p, 3d close. Make the same again, turn, ch 4d, skip a p of c-r, j to the next p. 4d. p, 4d, turn, make c-l each ring being. 3d-(p, 2d) 4 times, p, 3d, close, joining r by first and last p. Continue around clover with ch 3d-(p, 3d) twice, j to second p of ring last made on side 3d-(p, 3d) twice, j to top p of next r of c-l. Repeat from * once. Ch 3d-(p, 3d) 5 times, j to top p of first ring of c-l.*Ch 3d-(p, 3d) 5 times, j to top p of next r of c-l. Repeat from * once. Ch 3d-(p, 3d) 5 times, j to base of c-l, turn, Ch 4d, j to p of first inner straight ch, 4d, sk first p of c-r, j to next and repeat

Edge on Bottom. R 3d, p, 3d, j second p of ch of oblong, 3d, p, 3d, close. Turn, ch, 2d, (p, 2d) 5 times, turn.* R 3d-j last p of past ring, 3d j.next p of oblong, 3d, p, 3d, close, turn, ch 2d, (p, 2d) 5 times turn, repeat from *. Then a ring not joined to oblong and 2 more joined to oblong as shown, and a last one, after which, change shuttles, ch 4 d, p, 4d, change shuttles, and repeat from start of row.

Edge on Top. Like bottom edge, thro 7th ring, then turn, ch 4d-(p, 4d) 7 times j to p of last ch of bottom row-betw motifs. Turn ch 4d, j last p of long ch, (4d, j next p) 6 times, 4d, repeat from start.

Square in shoulder strap—r 2d-(p, 2d) 7 times, close. Change Shuttles * ch 4d, turn, r 3d, (p, 2d) 4 times, p 3d, close, repeat ring, turn, ch 4d sk a p of c-r and j to next p, repeat from * 3 times. Join threads at base of c-r tie and cut.

Edge—r 3d-(p, 2d) twice, j to last p of first r of sq also to first p of second ring. (2d, p) twice, 3d, close, turn ch 2d-(p, 2d) 5 times, j top of side ring of sq, ch 2d-(p, 2d) twice. 5 times. j to top of next ring of sq. Ch 2d-(p, 2d)5 times, turn. Ring 3d-(p, 2d) twice, j to last p of srme ring and to first p of next r. Complete ring and repeat from start. The other side edge is same, making ch of 4d-(p, 4d) 3 times, j at base of last r on other side edge, turn, ch 4d, join last p of ch just made, 4d-(j 4d) twice 4d and same edge.

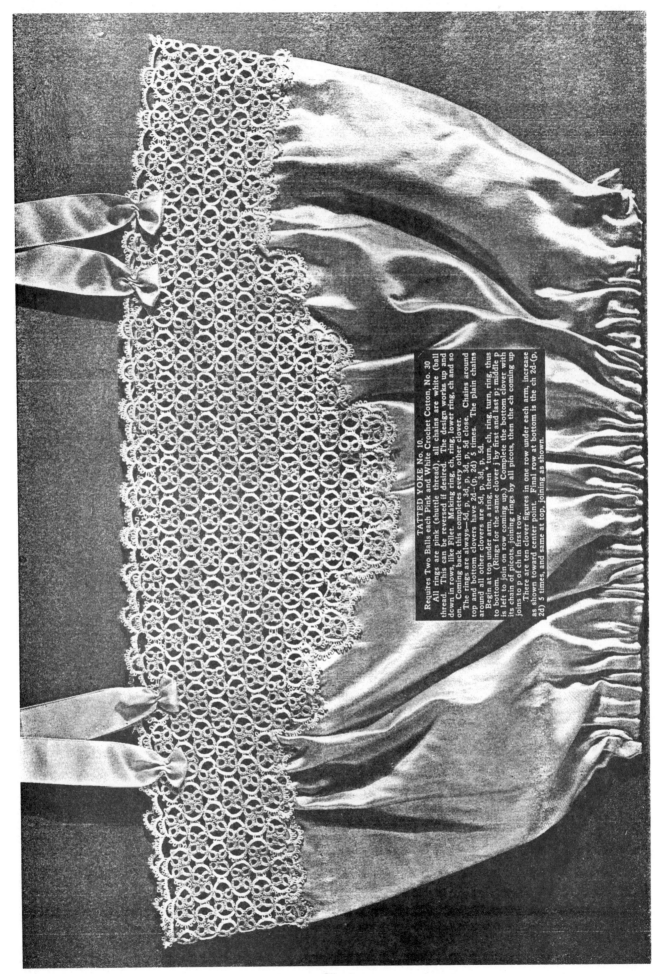

TATTED YOKE No. 10.

Requires Two Balls each Pink and White Crochet Cotton, No. 30

All rings are pink (shuttle thread), all chains are white (ball thread). This can be reversed if desired. The design works up and down in rows, like Filet. Making ring, ch, ring, lower ring, ch and so on. Coming back this completes every other clover.

The rings are always—5d, p, 3d, p, 3d, p, 5d close. Chains around top and bottom clovers have 2d—(p, 2d) 5 times. The plain chains around all other clovers are 5d, p, 3d, p, 5d.

Begin at top under arm, a ring, then * turn, ch, ring, turn, ring, thus to bottom. (Rings for the same clover j by first and last p; middle p is left to join on row coming up) Complete the bottom clover with its chain of picots, joining rings by all picots, then the ch coming up joins to p of ch in first row.

There are ten clover figures in one row under each arm, increase as shown toward center point. Final row at bottom is the ch 2d-(p, 2d) 5 times, and same at top, joining as shown.

86

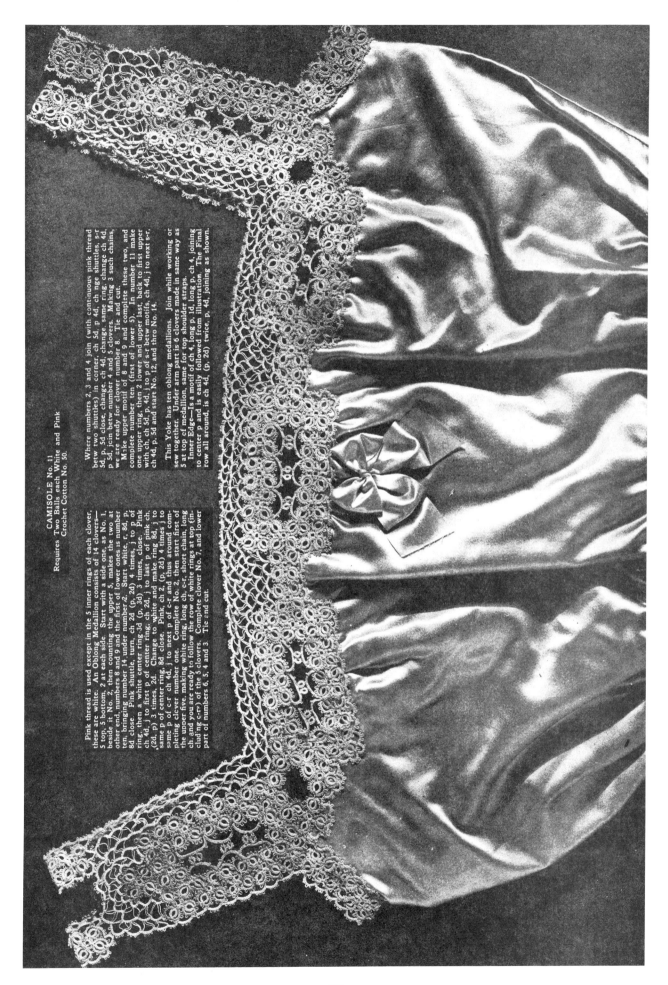

CAMISOLE No. 11

Requires Two Balls each White and Pink
Crochet Cotton No. 50.

Pink thread is used except in the 5 inner rings of each clover, these are white. An Oblong Medallion consists of 14 clovers— 5 top, 5 bottom, 2 at each side. Start with a side one, as No. 1, beside it No. 2, then counting the upper 5, makes the two at other end, numbers 8 and 9 and the first of lower ones is number ten, bringing number 14 under number 2. Start white, r, 8d, p, 8d close. Pink shuttle, turn, ch 2d (p, 2d) 4 times, j to p of ring, then a white center ring 3d (p, 3d) 3 times, close. Pink (2d, p) 3 times, 2d. Change to white and make ring 8d, j to same p of center ring, 8d close. Pink, ch 2, (p, 2d) 4 times, j to same p of c-r ch 4d, j to first p of center ring, ch 2d, j to last p of pink ch, same p of c-r ch 4d, j to next p of c-r and thus around completing clover number one. Complete No. 2, then start first of the upper five, making white ring, long ch, c-r, short chain, long ch and you are ready to follow the row of white rings at top (including c-rs) of the 5 clovers. Complete clover No. 7, and lower part of numbers 6, 5, 4 and 3. Tie and cut.

Where numbers 2, 3 and 4 join (with continuous pink thread betw two shuttles) in corner, ch 5d, p 4d, ch nge shuttles, s-r 5d, p, 5d close, change. ch 4d, change. same ring, change ch 4d, p 5d, join betw number 4 and 5 clovers. Making 3 such chains, we are ready for clover number 8. Tie and cut.

Make upper motif of 8 and 9 and complete these two, and complete number ten (first of lower 5). In number 11 make one upper ring, then 2 lower and upper last, back to first upper with ch 4d, p 5d, j to p of s-r betw motifs, ch 4d, j to next s-r, ch 4d, p, 5d and start No. 12 and thro No. 14.

This Yoke has ten oblong medallions. Join while working or sew together. Under arm part is 6 clovers made in same way as 5 at top of medallion, same for top shoulder straps.

Inner Edge—Is a motif of ch 4, long p, 1d, long p, ch 4, joining to center p and is easily followed from illustration. The Final row all around, is ch 4d, (p, 2d) twice, p, 4d, joining as shown.

87

TATTED YOKE No. 12.

Requires Two Balls No. 30 Crochet Cotton. Two Shuttles.

Begin in center with 4 ring motif. Ring 4d–(p, 4d) 3 times, close. Repeat ring 3 times joined on first and last p. Tie and cut.

First row around—with thread continuous betw shuttle and ball—join thread to p of first ring, ch 3d–(p, 2d) twice, p 3d, j where first and second rings joined, ch 3d–(p, 2d) twice, p 3d, j to p of next ring. Repeat, tie and cut.

Second row around—join thread to second p of first ch, ch 3d–(p, 2d) 4 times, p, 3d, j to middle p of next ch. Repeat, tie and cut.

Third row around—with thread continuous betw 2 shuttles, join thread to second p of first ch. Small ch, 4d, p 4d, j to 4th p of same ch turn work over, change shuttles, long ch, 4d–(p, 2d) 8 times, change shuttles, ring 2d–(p, 2d) 7 times, close, turn work over, change shuttles, ch 3d, p, 3d skip a p of ring, j to next. Ch 3d, p (this connects on adjoining scallop later) 3d, skipping a p of ring, j to next of ring ch 3d, p, 3 d, j at base of ring. (Ch 3d, p, 3d, skipping a p, join to next) this 4 times. Ch 4d, join to second p of next ch of row below, ch 4d, j to 4th p—of same ch, repeat, from * 7 times.

Make 20 medallions and arrange as shown. An edge can be adapted from a similar yoke in these pages if desired.

88

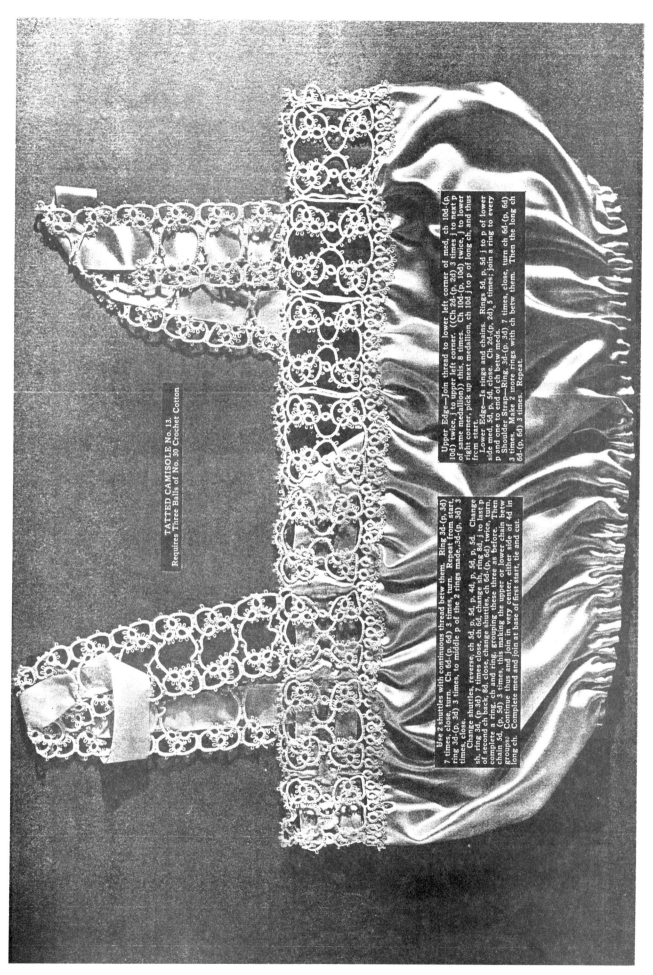

TATTED CAMISOLE No. 13.
Requires Three Balls of No. 30 Crochet Cotton

Use 2 shuttles with continuous thread betw them. Ring 3d-(p, 3d) 7 times, close, turn. Ch 6d-(p, 6d) 3 times, turn. Repeat from start, ring 3d-(p, 3d) 3 times, to middle p of the 2 rings made,-3d-(p, 3d) 3 times, close.

Change shuttles, reverse, ch 5d, p, 5d, p, 4d, p, 5d, p, 5d. Change sh, ring 3d, (p 3d) 7 times close, ch 6d, change sh, ring 8d, j to last p of second ch back, 8d, close, change shuttles, ch 6d-(p, 6d) twice, turn, complete a ring, ch and ring grouping these three as before. Then chain 5d, (p, 5d) 3 times, this making the upper or lower chain betw groups: Continue thus and join in very center, either side of 4d in long ch. Complete med and join at base of first start, tie and cut.

Upper Edge—Join thread to lower left corner of med, ch 10d-(p, 10d) twice, j to upper left corner. ((Ch 2d-(p, 2d) 3 times j to next p of same medallion)) this, 8 times. Ch 10d-(p, 10d) twice, j to lower right corner, pick up next medallion, ch 10d j to p of long ch, and thus from start.

Lower Edge—Is rings and chains. Rings 5d, p, 5d j to p of lower side med, 5d, p, 5d, close. Ch 2d-(p, 2d) 5 times; join a ring to every p and one to end of ch betw meds.

Shoulder Strap—Ring, 3d-(p, 3d) 7 times, close, turn ch 6d-(p, 6d) 3 times. Make 2 more rings with ch betw them. Then the long ch 6d-(p, 6d) 3 times. Repeat.

89

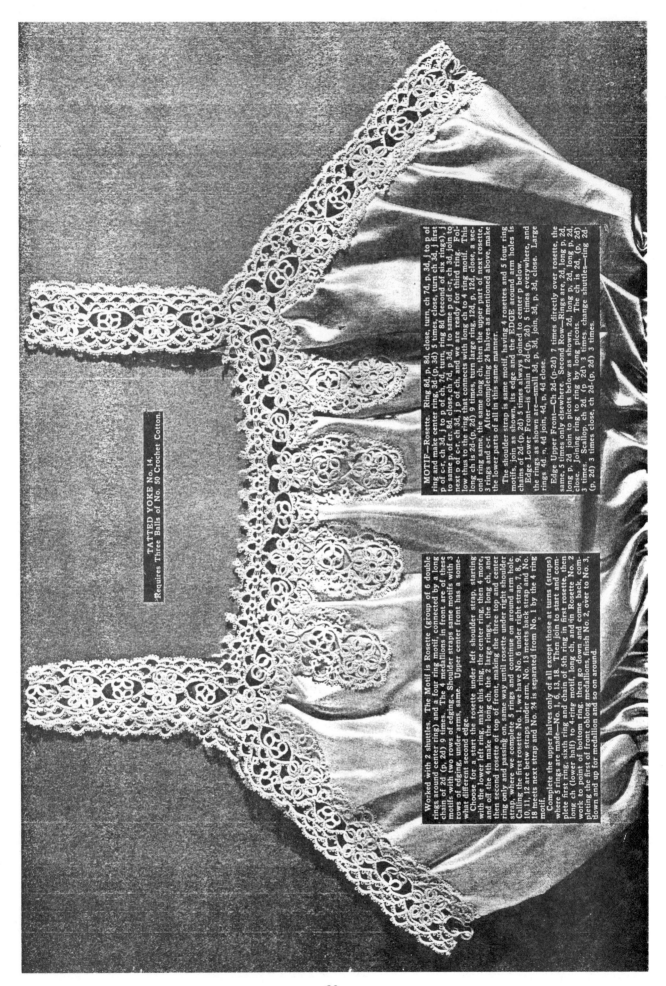

TATTED YOKE No. 14.
Requires Three Balls of No. 50 Crochet Cotton.

MOTIF—Rosette. Ring 8d, p, 8d, close, turn, ch 7d, p, 3d, j to p of ring and make center ring, 3d-(p, 3d) 5 times, close, turn ch 3d, j first p of c-r, ch 3d, j to p of ch, 7d, turn, ring 8d (second of six rings,) j to same p of cr, ch 8d, close, ch 7d, p 3d, j to same p of c-r, ch 3d, join to next p of c-r, ch 3d, j p of ch, and we are ready for third ring. Follow thus to the ring that connects with long ch to 4 ring motif. This long ch is 2d-(p, 2d) 9 times, turn large ring, 12d, p, 12d, close, a second ring same, the same long ch, then the upper part of next rosette, 3 rings and c-r. After completing 24 halves as mentioned above, make the lower parts of all in this same manner.

The shoulder strap is same motif, having 4 rosettes and 5 four ring motifs, join as shown, its edge and the EDGE around arm holes is chains of 2d-(p, 2d) 5 times always joined to center p below.

Edge Lower Front—is chain f 2d-(p, 2d) 5 times everywhere, and the rings as shown are—small 3d, p, 3d, join, 3d, p, 3d, close. Large rings 4d. n, 4d join, 4d, p, 4d close.

Edge Upper Front—Ch 2d-(p-2d) 7 times directly over rosette, the same, 5 times only elsewhere. Second Row—Rings are, 2d, long p, 2d, long p, 2d join to picots below as shown, 2d, long p, 2d, long p, 2d, close. Joining ring to ring by long picots. The ch is 2d, (p, 2d) 3 times. Scallop, ch 2d, (p, 2d) 3 times. change shuttles—ring 2d-(p, 2d) 3 times close, ch 2d-(p, 2d) 3 times.

Worked with 2 shuttles. The Motif is Rosette (group of 6 double rings around center ring) and a four ring motif, connected by a long chain of 2d (p, 2d) 9 times. The 4 medallions in front are of these motifs with two rows of edging. Shoulder straps same motifs with 3 rows of edging, under arms, same. Upper center front has a somewhat different second edge.

Choose for a start the rosette under left shoulder strap, starting with the lower left ring, make this ring, the center ring, then 4 more, and off the 4th make the long ch. the 2 large rings, the long ch, and then second rosette of top of front making the three top and center ring only and passing on, same way until rosette under right shoulder strap, where we complete 5 rings and continue on around arm hole. Calling the first rosette No. 1, we have No. 6 under right strap, 7, 8, 9, 10, 11, 12 are betw straps under arm, No. 13 meets back strap and No. 18 meets next strap and No. 24 is separated from No. 1 by the 4 ring motif.

Complete the upper halves only of all except those at turns (straps) where 5 rings are made—No. 1, 6, 13, 18. Then join to start and complete first ring, sixth ring and chain of 5th ring in first rosette, then long ch (lower half) to 4-ring motif, long ch, and in Rosette No. 2 work to point of bottom ring, then go down and come back, completing the first of front oblong medallions, finish No. 2, over to No. 3, down and up for medallion and so on around.

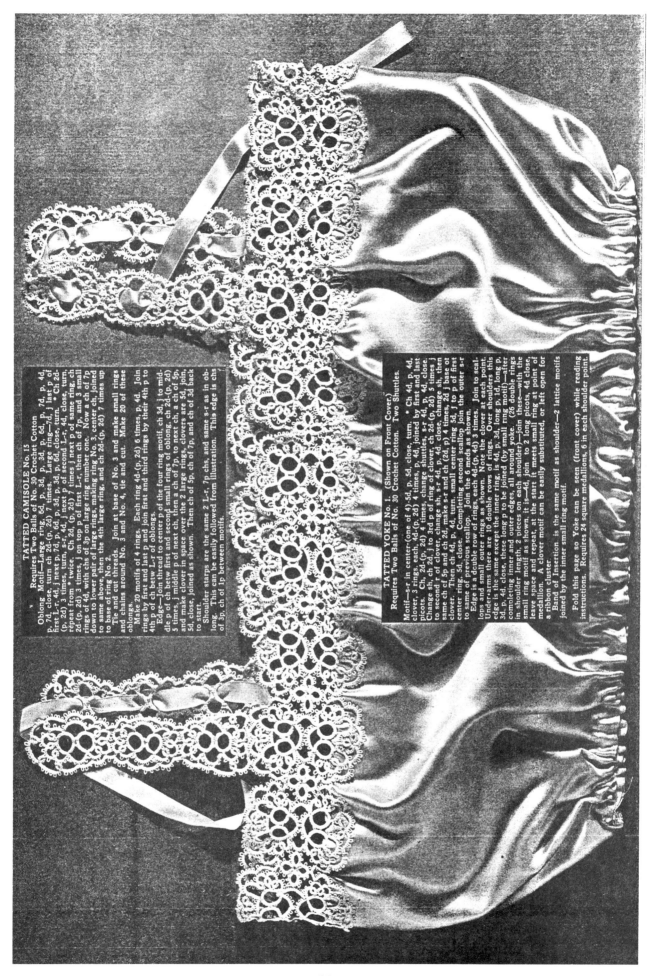

TATTED CAMISOLE No. 15

Requires Two Balls of No. 30 Crochet Cotton

Oblong Motif—Large ring, 6d, p, 3d, p, 3d, p, 6d, p, 7d, p, 4d, p, close, turn ch 2d-(p, 2d) 7 times. Large ring—7d, j last p of first L-r, 4d, j next p, 7d, p, 6d, p, 3d, p, 6d, close, turn, ** Ch 2d-(p, 2d) 3 times, turn, s-r, 4d, j next p of second L-r, 4d, close, turn, repeat from twice. Ch 2d, (p, 2d) 7 times j next p of same ring, ch 2d-(p, 2d) 3 times, j on top p of first L-r, then ch of 7p, and 3 small rings of 4d, with chs of 3p on large ring number one. Now a ch of 7p down to lower pair of large rings, making ring No. 3, center ch, joined to same above, then the 4th large ring, and ch 2d-(p, 2d) 7 times up to base of ring No. 2.

Tie and cut threads. Join at base of No. 3 and make small rings and chains around No. 3 and No. 4, tie and cut. Make 20 of these oblongs.

Make 20 motifs of 4 rings. Each ring 4d-(p, 2d) 6 times, p, 4d. Join rings by first and last p and join first and third rings by their 4th p to to 4th p of ch betw L-r of oblongs.

Edge—Join thread to center p of the four ring motif, ch 3d, j to middle p of ch betw first and second small rings of oblong, ch 2d-(p, 2d) 5 times, j middle p of next ch, then a ch of 7p, to next ch, a ch of 5p, and make clover in space over the 2 large rings, clovers are 5d, join, 5d, close, joined as shown. Then ch of 5p, ch of 7p, and ch of 3d back to start.

Shoulder starps are the same 2 L-r, 7p chs, and same s-r as in oblong. This can be easily followed from illustration. This edge is chs of 3p, ch of 1p between motifs.

TATTED YOKE No. 1. (Shown on Front Cover)

Requires Two Balls of No. 30 Crochet Cotton. Two Shuttles.

Motif—s-r in center—(one of 4)-5d, p, 5d, close, turn. * Ch 4d, 4d, clover, 3 rings, each, 4d-(p, 2d) 4 times, p, 4d, joined by first and last picots. Ch, 2d-(p, 2d) 4 times, change shuttles, s-r 4d, p, 4d, close. Change sh, ch 2d, j to 3rd p of ring of clover, ch 2d-(p, 2d) 5 times j to second r of clover, change sh, s-r 4d, p, 4d close, change sh, then same ch cf 5p and ch 2d, make s-r and ch (2d, p) 4 times, 2d j base of clover. Then ch 4d, p, 4d, turn, small center ring 5d, j to p of first center ring, 5d, close. Completing second scallop join the outer s-r to same of previous scallop. Join the 6 meds as shown.

Edge is a double row of rings, each 4d-(p, 4d) 3 times. Join to scallops and small outer rings as shown. Note the clover at each point. Underarms there are 10 double rows of rings. Over shoulders this edge is the same except the inner ring, is 4d, p, 3d, long p, 1d, long p, 3d, p, 4d, close, these long p to be joined (by small ring motif)—after completing inner and outer edges, all around yoke. (26 double rings in shoulder length, 2 pieces on each shoulder)—join these—with the small ring motif as shown, it is—4d, join to 2 long picots, 4d close, leave space and repeat, at the start it meets small ring at point of medallion. A clover motif can be easily substituted, or left open for a ribbon cluster.

Band of Insertion. is the same motif as shoulder—2 lattice motifs joined by the inner small ring motif.

Fold this page so Yoke can be seen (front cover) while reading instructions. Requires 24 square medallions, 6 in each shoulder point.

LACIS publishes and distributes books specifically related to the textile arts, focusing on the subject of lace and lace making, costume, embroidery, needlepoint and hand sewing.

Other LACIS books of interest:

NEW DIMENSIONS IN TATTING, To de Haan-van Beek

PRACTICAL TATTING, Phyllis Sparks

THE ART OF TATTING, Katherine Hoare

TATTING WITH VISUAL PATTERNS, Mary Konior

TATTING; Designs From Victorian Lace, Ed by Jules & Kaethe Kliot

THE COMPLETE BOOK OF TATTING, Rebecca Jones

BEAD EMBROIDERY, Joan Edwards

EMBROIDERY WITH BEADS, Angela Thompson

BEAD EMBROIDERY, Valerie Campbell-Harding and Pamela Watts

BEAD WORK, Ed. Jules & Kaethe Kliot

THE BEADING BOOK, Julia Jones

THE BARGELLO BOOK, Frances Salter

FLORENTINE EMBROIDERY, Barbara Muller

ARMENIAN LACE, Nouvart Tashjian

BATTENBERG AND POINT LACE, Nellie Clarke Brown

NEEDLE LACES: BATTENBERG, POINT & RETICELLA, 2nd Ed., Jules & Kaethe Kliot

CUTWORK, HEDEBO & BRODERIE ANGLAISE, Ed., Jules & Kaethe Kliot

TRADITIONAL DESIGNS IN HARDANGER EMBROIDERY, Ed. Jules & Kaethe Kliot

LACE NET EMBROIDERY, EMBROIDERY ON TULLE AND NET, Th. De Dillmont

THE NEEDLE-MADE LACES OF RETICELLA, Jules & Kaethe Kliot

TENERIFFE LACE, Jules & Kaethe Kliot

THE ART OF NETTING, Ed. Jules & Kaethe Kliot

IRISH CROCHET LACE: INSTRUCTIONS AND DESIGNS, Ed. Jules & Kaethe Kliot

THE ART OF SHETLAND LACE, Sarah Don

KNITTED LACE, Marie Niedner & Gussi von Reden

THE KNITTED LACE PATTERNS OF CHRISTINE DURCHOW, Vol I, Jules & Kaethe Kliot

THE CARE AND PRESERVATION OF TEXTILES, Karen Finch & Greta Putnam

THE ART OF DRAWN WORK (1896), Butterick Publishing Co.

MAGIC OF FREE-MACHINE EMBROIDERY, Doreen Curran

SINGER INSTRUCTIONS FOR ART EMBROIDERY AND LACE WORK, Singer Sewing Machine Co.

SMOCKING AND GATHERING FOR FABRIC MANIPULATION, Nellie Weymouth Link

MILLINERY FOR EVERY WOMAN, Georgina Kerr Kaye

DRAFTING AND PATTERN DESIGNING, Woman's Institute of Domestic Arts & Sciences

FASHION OUTLINES, Margaret C. Ralston

GARMENT PATTERNS FOR THE EDWARDIAN LADY, Mrs. F.E. Thompson

"STANDARD" WORK ON CUTTING (MEN'S GARMENTS): 1886, Jno. J. Mitchell Co.

LADIES' TAILOR-MADE GARMENTS 1908, S.S. Gordon

THE ART & CRAFT OF RIBBON WORK, Ed by Jules & Kaethe Kliot

THE ART OF HAIR WORK, HAIR BRAIDING AND JEWELRY OF SENTIMENT (1875), Mark Campbell

For a complete list of LACIS titles write to:

LACIS
3163 Adeline Street
Berkeley, CA 94703
USA